VINTAGE SOPER

Also by Brian Frost

Goodwill on Fire: Donald Soper's Life and Mission

Vintage Soper

God, Faith and Society

Edited and arranged by Brian Frost

Hodder & Stoughton
LONDON SYDNEY AUCKLAND

Introduction and editorial matter
copyright © Brian Frost, 1997
Illustrations copyright © Philip Spence, 1997

First published in Great Britain 1997

The right of Brian Frost to be identified as the Author of
the Work has been asserted by him in accordance with the
Copyright, Designs and Patents Act 1988.

1 3 5 7 9 10 8 6 4 2

British Library Cataloguing in Publication Data
A record for this book is available from the British Library

ISBN 0 340 66516 5

Typeset by Hewer Text Composition Services, Edinburgh
Printed and bound in Great Britain
by Clays Ltd, St Ives plc

Hodder and Stoughton
A Division of Hodder Headline PLC
338 Euston Road
London NW1 3BH

Contents

Preface

This collection of the main ideas I have sown in many fields has been culled from over six decades of writing and speaking, broadcasting and preaching. It gives an indication of the theology which has shaped my actions, but because I have always been more a prospector than a pronouncer when it comes to ultimate truth you will find in *Vintage Soper* guidelines rather than goalposts.

Moreover, in a public life which has involved me in speaking about belief in God 'on the run', so to speak, it was often not possible to top and tail comments and reflections about Christian faith and life. So you will find here rough-and-ready approaches to problems rather than a systematic theology. Readers should also bear in mind that, like those of other thinkers, my convictions may have been modified and expanded in the light of new evidence, more insight and increasing experience of life. Nevertheless, I do offer this volume as a reasonable expression of my perceptions in words about the Christian faith as I have tried, however haltingly, to respond to the problems and complexities of the twentieth century.

I remain convinced, of course, that our main response must always be one of discipleship in the midst of the daily paradoxes, ambiguities and tensions which confront each of us. Latterly, I have had to wrestle with the meaning of my discipleship in the context of ageing, an experience which has led me to reflect on the spiritual resources I needed as my discipleship moved into a different gear. I have had to come to terms with the uneven process of ageing and on the emotional level have tried to remember the past without remorse. Rather I have endeavoured to recall previous experiences in a way which brings pleasure.

The Church too has sustained me in its fellowship. Indeed, I have been fortunate because I have been able to continue a ministry of Word and Sacrament, as well as outdoor speaking, broadcasting and lecturing, well into my nineties. Of course, some of the battles of previous decades no longer rage; some of the storms have died away; and some of the problems with which I wrestled earlier are now out of date.

I have come to realise that old people are special precisely because of their longevity. Yet to arrange for their adequate care is by no means easy. As I wrote in the journal *Care of the Elderly* in April 1990: 'In this present world of regular sinners with seasonal bursts of unselfishness, I find the need for communal care, as administered by society acting as a whole, is the priority requirement. Whatever socialism may mean as a political programme for public administration, I am more than ever convinced that the care of the aged is a priority that can only effectively be accepted and enforced by the community acting as a whole.'

But adequate physical care is not enough. We need a spirituality, one of the main aspects of which must surely be a sense of humour, which can play a therapeutic role. For, as I wrote in another article for *Care of the Elderly*, in July 1990: 'To regard the oddities of daily life as a cause of amusement when they no longer seem capable of reconciliation takes the edge off exasperation. It can sweeten sorrow too.'

My humour has been occasional, in the exact sense of that word. Preparing jokes and deliberately inserting them into a public speech can be a dangerous course to take. At the same time, if treated with care, humour can be an all-important ingredient, especially if it emerges from the immediacy of what is written or, in the open air, spoken.

One of the first questions I was asked when I began open-air speaking was 'What shape is your soul when dead?' I replied, 'Oblong. Next question.' On another occasion a heckler, knowing Methodists could be narrow-minded, asked 'Can Methodists dance?' to which I replied (echoing the Revd Russell Maltby, who first said it), 'Some can and some can't.' I was caught, however, by another heckler when I suggested to him that when St Paul said, 'Take a little wine for your stomach's sake,' he was advising his questioner to rub it in. I tried another route by indicating that in the Psalms wine was described as 'a mocker' and that drink could have quite strong effects. 'Good,' the heckler responded. 'I've been looking for that sort of stuff for the last twenty years.'

I have valued humour as a part of spirituality all my life. The legacy I received from my family – radicalism from my mother and a strong Puritan ethic from my father – was tempered by what I came to regard as a cockney component, which enabled me to say things in lively ways. Taken out of context, of course, witty or funny remarks can seem less pungent when repeated on the printed page, but in *Vintage Soper* some have been included between sections to give the flavour of the style I developed over many years.

Humour, of course, is not the only spiritual quality God has implanted in men and women. There is also the sense of beauty and a love of poetry and music. These enable us to catch a glimpse of an eternal realm here on earth as we pursue our discipleship to the end and are above all politics, all campaigning, all preaching and oratory. There is, as I once wrote in the November 1961 edition of *Sanity*, the journal of the Campaign for Nuclear Disarmament, no other through road but political action, even though it is 'a long, desperate, continuously disappointing road'. Yet always transcending politics is this other world which also summons us and where we can find refreshment, whether through families and friends, worship and adoration or wonder at the mysteries of science and religion that lie all about us.

Donald Soper

Introduction

Donald Soper's Twentieth-century Journey

From the time Donald Soper went to Oakley Place Methodist Church, just off the Old Kent Road in south London, in the autumn of 1926, he was seldom out of the spotlight either in his own or other churches and, later, in the press and on radio and television. How did he stand the glare of so much publicity, so much attention and so much controversy as his remarks and views often caused his hearers and readers either to oppose him strongly or to support and defend him vigorously?

His undoubted strength came not only from an outstanding intellect and a photographic memory, which enabled him to pluck out of the air material for speeches and sermons, but also from deep-rooted convictions and perceptions. These he wrote about in detail only once, in the Methodist Lent Book for 1956, *All His Grace*. But a study of his other books, sermons, talks, broadcasts and off-the-cuff remarks reveals a well-thought-out Christian position that was the root both of his radical concerns and of his political activities as he tried to live out a pioneer ministry of great originality.

When Donald was young the ecumenical movement was in its infancy and being influenced in Britain by William Temple, later Archbishop of Canterbury, and Professor R. H. Tawney, of the London School of Economics, whom Donald met only once near the end of Tawney's life, when the Christian Socialist Movement was formed in 1960. Both shaped his thinking, the former through his *Readings in St John's Gospel*, the latter through his two books *Religion and the Rise of Capitalism* and *The Acquisitive Society*.

Parallel to this development, as the Churches of the world tried to come together in new ways, both for social action and in unity, was the increasing importance of science. In the early part of the century Einstein, with his theory of relativity, and Heisenberg, with his theory of uncertainty, had made their discoveries; now decades later other scientists argued about the mystery at the heart of matter and the theory of black holes.

Donald Soper was extremely aware of the impact these and other scientific developments had on Christian faith and wrestled continually with the effect of scientific truth on the traditional formulations of Christian belief. Because of his sensitivity to his environment he was also alert to the growth of secularism and its erosion of church life and witness.

He was aware, as he often said, that he was living in 'the first secular age in history'[1] and therefore, unlike other evangelists before him, who could assume some knowledge of Christianity, tried to present a coherent faith for that society, as the decades of doubt went by, in less theological language. Moreover, as he scanned the world, and as his travels to most continents made him unusually aware of the global village in which human beings increasingly lived after 1945, he could not fail to notice the economic and political revolutions which were in train as the developing world made its critique of the West. He was aware too that Marxist-influenced governments, both in Eastern Europe and in China, were seeking to solve in new ways endemic problems of poverty and equality which Donald knew capitalism had failed to solve during its centuries of dominance.

The Context of Donald Soper's Ministry

'The first thing to do about the divisions of the Christian Church is to be ashamed of them, and I am,' he wrote in 1953.[2] Already in 1949, just after the Amsterdam Assembly of the World Council of Churches in 1948, he had called for unity between all of the Christian faith.[3] But he was never formally involved with the World Council; he was a Methodist delegate to its 1954 Evanston Assembly but had to leave before it had properly begun because his father was ill.

Nevertheless, Donald nearly always talked in an ecumenical context while making his audiences aware that he was a Methodist minister and proud of it. Indeed, with his great emphasis on love, which he tried to apply both to individuals and to society, he was in a tradition which could be traced back to John Wesley himself, who had declared there was no holiness but social holiness.

'What is desperately needed is that Christians of every denomination, and Roman Catholics especially, should make the strongest efforts to worship together,' he wrote in 1956. 'Methodists should know the Mass, just as I hope Roman Catholics would know something about Methodist love-feasts.'[4] For him the Roman Catholic Church, which had 'more saints per square yard than every other church',[5] was the 'supreme historical realisation of Christianity'.[6] But it needed to 'take on board the Methodists some time, drop the word Roman, come to terms with the word Catholic'.[7] 'Of course there's a Catholic Church,' he added, 'and I am a member of it.'[8]

On other occasions he showed his appreciation of the Society of Friends. 'The Quakers are nearer to institutional Christianity than anybody I know,' he judged.[9] As for Methodism itself, which had cradled and nurtured him, and whose churches and halls he knew so intimately, he did not doubt it had been born to fulfil 'a genuine Christian purpose'[10] but felt as a separate institution 'it ought to die to rise into a new and larger Christianity.'[11] He was clear that its role in Britain was to be a preaching order within the Church of England, for that was where its origins lay.

Donald wished the ecumenical movement were stronger and especially that the Pope would declare unambiguously that war was wrong. Yet he was equally clear that 'no one church has a monopoly of goodness, theology or common sense.'[12] If, therefore, Christians were to come together, it had to be 'by doing the same thing rather than saying the same thing'.[13]

If, on the one hand, Donald spoke within the context of ecumenical Christianity – after his visit to Russia in 1956 this included the Eastern Orthodox Church too – he also spoke within the context of empiricism and scientific truth, which had its own rules and whose insights he related to truth as mediated through the Bible, the Church and its saints. This was because he was in the tradition of philosophical theology which he had first come across through the writings and lectures of F. R. Tennant when he was an undergraduate at Cambridge University in the 1920s. Later he also came under the influence of the seventeenth-century French thinker Blaise Pascal and, latterly, of Professor Hans Kung, the Roman Catholic theologian and writer.

Donald Soper's aim was clear: to help ordinary men and women wrestle with the great theological, personal, social and political issues of the century, which he tried to explain in straightforward language, even though the *implications* of what he was saying were often far from straightforward. 'The moment you say why, you are in the realm of purpose, not of fact,' he once observed in Hyde Park, to be told by a member of the crowd he was very Cartesian.[14] On another occasion there he suggested that when he asked himself 'Why should there be anything at all?' he was driven to the conclusion that there had to be something behind the universe of a non-physical nature, 'otherwise you can't make sense of it'.[15] Belief in God he found had progressively answered more questions for him than any other belief, though it could never answer all life's mysteries.[16]

Donald always tried to start where people were rather than with abstract questions like the traditional arguments for the existence of God. He was convinced too that people needed to know the meaning of the physical world if they were to know the meaning of the spiritual.[17] So he tended often to present Christianity first and foremost in the context of bread-and-butter issues. 'The good news,' he maintained, 'begins where the need is most obvious';[18] and in his role as an evangelist he tried to awaken people to a vision of a world renewed by the impact of the Christian faith. 'The technique of evangelism,' he once explained, 'is to produce a picture of the kingdom of God, and then to awaken the enthusiasm of those who are prepared so to be dedicated, and so to be disciplined, and so to deny themselves, as to be its pioneers. It is they who will blaze its trail.'[19]

He sketched his approach in greater detail at a Home Mission meeting in the Victoria Hall, Bolton, in 1952 when he maintained: 'Unless our evangelism is rooted in the experience of the heart and the enrichment of the mind, it will not reach the masses of our day. Only if our evangelism is aggressive in its advocacy of peace, the needs of the community and the economic conditions which belong to the full life, linked up with our prayers, will it meet the needs of the age, conforming to Christ's claim that the kingdoms of this world will become the kingdoms of his great kingdom.'[20]

But whereas some wanted the overthrow of outworn systems by revolutions engineered by violence, Donald saw clearly the contradictory nature on which such an attitude to change rested. He aimed, therefore, to seek a kingdom where God's grace reigned, acting in the life both of individuals and of groups, large and small. 'We need a moral revolution,' was his cry. 'An act of penitence for our disobedience to God whose guidance and grace alone fit us to use aright the gifts and good things with which he has filled his universe.'[21]

He never wavered from this position, though he was always ready to join with his secular and agnostic friends in the Labour Party, and indeed beyond it, over particular causes and when they needed general support. Sometimes, of course, the issues which galvanised him, like teetotalism or pacifism or his left-wing political views, made him unpopular with now this, now that constituency with which he was engaged. Indeed, it is true to say that while most people liked some aspect of Donald's approach to Christianity, few liked all.

His evangelism, and indeed his pre-evangelism, for such it was – a preparation for the word of grace, as Dietrich Bonhoeffer called the latter – was twofold. At the intellectual level Donald aimed to help people grapple with how faith and the scientific world view could coexist in a creative tension. At the revolutionary level he sought to convince his hearers about not metaphysics but ethics. Indeed, he had few pretensions to being a theologian. 'Theology is an exercise in illustration, not in definition and not even in description,' he explained.[22] 'It is essentially an art form not a scientific thesis.' He once told a friend, George Hunter, that one of the reasons why he emphasised ethics was because he was 'more profoundly suspicious of metaphysics'.[23]

Similarly, Donald was not interested in the minutiae of biblical criticism and the nuances of passages of Scripture. The Sermon on the Mount, for example, which so captivated him, was not 'to be analysed or qualified but obeyed', Gordon Wakefield considers. 'For him the Sermon contains the doctrine which took Jesus to the cross.'[24] Jesus, for Donald Soper, took his disciples into his confidence and offered them 'as Garibaldi offered his warriors and patriots a hundred years ago, an adventure much of which is as yet unknown and shadowy, but an adventure in which he believes. "And I, if I be lifted up, will draw all people to myself."'[25]

The Content of His Ministry

As Donald presented Jesus, he was always the man whose life of non-violence and of love led inexorably from Galilee to Jerusalem and to the crucifixion. If the Catholic in Donald Soper made him want both to value and commend eucharistic devotion and practice, the evangelical, if such a distinction can be validly made, meant he focused on Christ's cross. His understanding of this was particularly evident at the Good Friday Three Hours' Devotion, both at Kingsway Hall and latterly at Hinde Street Methodist Church, when he talked about Jesus's forgiveness, offered to all, as he accomplished God's purpose of salvation. 'To forgive when there is much to be forgiven is one thing,' he explained one Good Friday, 'but to forgive in the innocence of one's life and the cruelty and wickedness of the assertions of guilt that were heaped upon him is another, a unique expression of what forgiveness at its heart means.'[26]

With his understanding of God's forgiveness, revealed through Christ's cross, Donald linked his clear and continued conviction that families were the most useful theological model for understanding God's actions in Jesus Christ, despite the obvious brokenness of many of them. Meditating on Jesus's words 'Woman, behold thy son . . . Behold thy mother!' he once suggested it was important to realise the significance of Jesus's reported words for an understanding not only of the role of woman, and especially of Mary, but also of the Church as a family. From there, for Donald, it was but a short jump to understanding the entire human race as God's family, within which the Church had a specific ministry, because Jesus had died for all. Certainly that was the inner motivation which led him to take missions in Africa and the Americas and, at the height of the Cold War, to make a number of visits to Eastern Europe.

He spelt out his inner motivation most clearly in 1980, when he indicated that he thought most people knew something of the love of a mother or father, sister or brother and could recognise actions contrary to such roles. 'We are made for that kind of relationship,' he continued, 'however much we may err or transgress. I believe that the future of human beings does depend – and this is no grandiose simplification – on the extension of that which Jesus offered to the whole human race.'[27]

Donald Soper did not think human beings could abandon religion without courting drastic consequences. Yet he did not want them to abuse religion by escaping from the problems of the twentieth century (indeed, for him, healthy religion could act against the development of psychosis). Rather he wanted men and women to 'use religion not as a way out of problems but as a way into solutions'.[28] That was why he spent so many hours offering Christ to what Gordon Wakefield has called 'our gadget-ridden society'[29] with an almost Franciscan-like simplicity – to crowds and passers-by, to congregations and listeners and viewers. So to the mainly secular, if not agnostic, readers of *Tribune* he wrote a few days after the assassination of Martin Luther King in Memphis, Tennessee, on 4 April 1968: 'Holy Week and Passion-tide proclaim the ultimate victory not of violence, but of non-violence. At the foot of the cross on Good Friday, the way of Jesus, of Gandhi, of Martin Luther King may look like defeat, but Good Friday is not the end of the Christian year, only its beginning. The end is Easter morning when even death is swallowed up in victory, and we sing:

> The strife is o'er – the battle done
> Now is the victor's triumph won.[30]

Again, in Hyde Park twenty-five years later, as he tried to reinterpret the Christian doctrine of the resurrection for a secular crowd, he declared that Jesus was 'demonstrating the ultimate victory of life over death'.[31] Jesus had not physically risen from the dead body when he came back but was in a body looking largely like the former physical body. That indomitable victory of life over death, he added, we can inherit, both as proposition and as hope.

'The real essence of the Christian life is not in success but in faithfulness,'[32] he told another listening crowd, aware, as in the late 1930s when he took an unpopular pacifist position and encouraged others to do the same, that Christianity was more like the mustard seed and the leaven in Jesus's parable, producing changed lives, which in due course would transform the world.

It was, of course, deep theological conviction which made Donald Soper look around for a political movement with which to ally himself, as well as his emotional response to the General Strike of 1926 and the poverty he witnessed in south London and elsewhere thereafter. 'When I was young,' he once confessed when in his eighties, 'socialism was the light of my life.'[33] He never wavered from this conviction because essentially he was trying to live out in a concrete setting a theology rooted in the doctrine of the Church – and its mission, especially in terms of the kingdom of God – in contemporary society. As a result, there had to be compromise along the way, for he could not stand by and, as an onlooker, refuse to get his hands dirty with twentieth-century agonies. The only questions, therefore, were: what was a legitimate compromise, and what were his Christian and political priorities?

The Communication of His Message

How did Donald Soper set about communicating his message? Fortunately, he had been given by nature an attractive personality and a temperament more Cavalier than Roundhead, though ethically he was more Roundhead than Cavalier. Like the four Gospel writers and compilers themselves, he was often a storyteller, weaving truth into his stories as he went, some of which over the years acquired myths and elaborations, so many times were they recounted.

He once attempted to explain the doctrine of the atonement

by talking about a proving flight he was on from Australia to Britain. Had he known that the purpose of the flight was to achieve the journey in a certain period of time, he doubted that he would have clambered on board, but once on the plane he had to trust the pilot, he explained to his congregation. Eventually the pilot landed the plane safely in London and he imagined both pilot and airline officials saying, 'It is finished.' Not that flights between Australia and Britain were at an end, he went on, but the way was now open for many more, though there could never be another proving flight. 'I think of Jesus,' he concluded. 'He has made the proving flight. There are still hazards to overcome and, I dare say, all kinds of difficulties to be faced, but the journey can now be undertaken. The kingdom of Heaven is open. He has opened the gate. In that sense his work is finished.'[34]

One of Donald's gifts as speaker and preacher was to take illustrations from his own experience and relate them to deeper truths in a way which made his audience listen to him most attentively. He once wanted to help his listeners come to a greater sense of marvel and did this by describing an experience he had during his Russian visit. He had been to a museum in Moscow, he explained, and had seen there metalwork dug out of the Caucasus the size of a pea and of golden texture. As he peered at it through a telescope, he saw 'a patterned and beautiful festooned bouquet of flowers'.[35] 'I shall never forget,' he added, 'the sense of awe and wonder at the thought of some primitive man . . . fashioning that thing of eternal beauty.'[36] Also striking was the way he helped children to understand Christ in one of his broadcasts in the BBC's *Children's Hour*, when he explained that the skyscrapers of New York were safe, even in difficult conditions, because the rock of Manhattan Island on which they were built was all of a piece and the engineers had done their work properly. Similarly, he had found that his life was safe if he built on the words of Jesus.

> To believe that I am God's child, that he loves me, that Jesus is my Saviour and friend, and that I, too, can love and serve people like he did, and so try to live every day as he wants me to live, that is to build my life up to the heights. And I know that while my faith and hope are up in the clouds like the tops of those skyscrapers, yet underneath is the rock; and because the foundations are firm, my faith cannot be blown away, and my hopes for the coming of God's kingdom can stand up to the fiercest storms.[37]

Just after war had been declared in the autumn of 1939 he wanted to explain how God could take people and shape them for service. There was a grandeur about his theme and he needed to excite his listeners about the greatness of God. His mind went back to his visit to South Africa at the invitation of a friend in 1937 and the story of the Great Trek which the Afrikaners had undertaken in the nineteenth century as men, women and children left the places where they had been born for unknown territory and futures. Their ruggedness and faith had impressed him when he heard about their story, he indicated, with their 'concept of religion that God had made a city for them and God would care for them' as they demonstrated they were 'people of the way'.[38] His hearers were left in no doubt that he hoped British Christians would have a like faith in the trials which were about to descend on them.

Donald Soper nearly always took August off for his annual holiday with his family, often in Cornwall, whose coastline especially he came to love. It also provided him with further illustrative material. On the Christian pilgrimage, he taught in the mid-1950s, there was 'much darkness and mist, just as, looking out of a window in Cornwall yesterday, one moment you could see the horizon, with the cliffs and the sea and the surf, and the next moment, the mist had come down and you could see no further than a few yards from your window'.[39]

He used another Cornish experience to help his congregation understand the physical world in which they were living and the kind of God in whom they believed. 'I remember once at Bedruthven steps,' he began, 'retiring behind a rock to get ready to bathe, and the tide was just going out. Behind that rock, left by the receding tide, was a little pool. I suppose there are millions of such pools; I remember this one. It was glistening in the sunlight. There was the ripple of miniature waves and in it were stones and rocks and tiny creatures – an ocean in miniature. They tell me that that which belongs to the realm of smaller things – the atom . . . perceptibly obeys the same kind of laws as do the greatest and most enormous constellations of the heavens.'[40]

Uniquely, Donald was able to communicate the truths he had within him by the use of what some have dubbed 'Soperisms', pithy and often aphoristic ways of saying things which both arrested the mind and lodged in it long after Donald himself had forgotten what he had said or where he had said it. Sometimes these were his own creations; sometimes they had been coined by others, like 'If you can make sure of the humanity of Jesus, his divinity will look after itself,'[41] which he had heard William Temple say. Even in Donald's homilies at the ten o'clock Eucharist at Hinde Street Methodist Church in the 1990s, when in his ninety-second year, he was on occasions still capable of Soperisms like 'No one proceeds in absolute innocence to the annunciation of justice for others.'[42]

In his writing and his speaking, penetrating comments were a regular, not an occasional, feature of his style. Thus, in 1947, 'The Christian Revolution means loving your enemy into friendship and loving your neighbour into fellowship'[43] and, in 1970, 'The very accusations that men and women make against the Church are more or less unconscious tributes to the character of its founder.'[44] Again, 'All true religion begins in gratitude'[45] and perhaps one of his best, written in 1989, 'Remorse is penitence sterilised against hope.'[46] Two Soperisms in particular sum up his perception about the twentieth century, one spoken when he was sixty-four, 'We're far too clever by half and not good enough by a mile',[47] the other when he was ninety, 'Our age is one which possesses adequate truth but insufficient grace.'[48]

Part of the power of Donald's technique of communication lay in his teaching ability. So when he came to talk about sin, a subject twentieth-century men and women were often reluctant to acknowledge, he made his hearers sit up and take note of what he was saying because of the attractive and unusual way he phrased his thoughts on the subject. So 'Sin is the second strongest thing in the universe but the love of God is stronger'[49] and, as he put it on Tower Hill in a more secular way, 'Sin is nearly as strong as goodness.'[50]

'I preach against sin,' he once told hearer and heckler alike at Hyde Park. 'I'm in no danger of being out of work.'[51] But what was sin? 'Sin is the malignant use of our freedom,' he explained.[52] But where would human beings be if they did not have to struggle to be and do good? 'I have never believed,' he made clear, 'the absence of temptation leads to the divine qualities of saintliness.'[53]

14

When he wanted to teach people the difference between abhorrence of wrongdoing and the correct attitude to wrong-doers, he said pithily, 'Hating sinners is bad; hating sin is good.'[54] And when he wanted to espouse the need for just systems as well as to applaud individuals who were charitable, he declared: 'Occasional generosity is no substitute for regular justice.'[55] Perhaps one of his most arresting sayings, which sums up both the subtlety and the clarity of his mind, occurred in Hyde Park in 1976 as he proclaimed, 'A great many aspects of Marx are incompatible with Christianity. A great many things Christians say are incompatible with what Jesus said.'[56]

The Core of His Message

Because Donald was convinced that the twentieth century's secularism needed to find religious roots if it was ever to produce lasting fruits worthy of its aspirations, he devoted all his energies and intellect to promoting and polishing his message as he adapted his style to a sceptical and mass-media age. Spurning those who disliked reason as a tool and who feared doubt or sought theological systems which were neatly packaged, he yet tried to explain there was a mystery at the heart of creation itself which ultimately no words could explain, or do justice to, though he himself caught glimpses of that mystery in love and in great music, whether classical or jazz.

Seeing himself as a knight of old on a quest for the celestial city, he often of course became battle-scarred and weary but knew he could find refreshment in the Church's fellowship and worship, especially at its Eucharist, which he liked to celebrate weekly. His Christology and metaphysic (for he did have one, though in heated moments in the open air and elsewhere he tended to deny this) helped him too, rooted as they were in the Gospels. The Epistles and the Book of Revelation were referred to less by him, and he missed the subtleties which later biblical scholarship found in the unity of the Old and New Testaments, but he never tired of proclaiming Jesus Christ as friend, brother, pioneer and forerunner, as well as Saviour and Lord.

In the quest for the historical Jesus, which most Christians in some measure pursue – for, as Donald saw clearly, Christianity is historical or it is nothing – he put his weight behind a human Jesus rather than the supernatural being of much later theology and Church history. If questioned about his authority for this, he would in the last resort have to admit it was his own judgment, informed by study and reading and, he hoped, inspired by the Holy Spirit. In that, he was more a Protestant than a Catholic Christian, for all his understanding of the two thousand years of Church history and his tendency to ride roughshod over painstaking research by the world's biblical scholars from many backgrounds.

Maintaining, as he did, a healthy tension between Church and Kingdom, seen in later years often in the context of eternity, there was a certain logic in the way he linked sacramentalism, pacifism, socialism and evangelism, for each, in his view, supported and affected the others. They formed a unified world vision and did not stand independently of each other. There was therefore, in Donald's opinion, little point in espousing pacifism unless it was linked with a political conviction which yearned for a different economic and social order. Yet politics 'unscaffolded' was unable to fertilise community life unless politicians were deeply rooted in a sacramental dimension where the grace of God shaped them through eucharistic worship.

As far back as the 1930s he had been convinced philosophically that materialism was a barren creed, though personally he valued the Marxist insight into the way economic forces shaped the lives of communities. His vision of Jesus Christ, therefore, was of a man who was down to earth and practical, caring for the needs of the ordinary people and healing them too. This, therefore, became the starting-point for Donald Soper's preaching. In that sense he was optimistic, and he did believe the world could become a better place despite the sin which affected it everywhere and which he found a constant menace. He encouraged others to espouse his 'optimism of grace', as Methodist theology has sometimes been termed, to follow him into the public arena and to become mature in faith. In his view, they would need the virtues of obedience, perseverance, faithfulness and a certain doggedness in the face of adversity for this. But Christians could achieve holiness because they followed one who was moral exemplar rather than judge and whose spirit was now available to empower them.

Donald, of course, like most thinkers, had certain presuppositions which underpinned his actions. There was, for example, the need he felt to struggle with, and wrestle for, the truth, from whichever quarter it came. There was the tension too between the secular and the sacred to be considered and a balance to be maintained between the personal and the social.

Moreover, in his view, Christians should stop apologising for Jesus Christ, not be afraid of fallibility and not claim too much. Rather they should seek to present the Christian gospel in new ways. He hoped, as he attempted to lead the way, that some of the barriers which had been erected between the Church and the contemporary world would be overcome.

When Donald first started to think about these issues he was seized, as were many liberal Protestants, by the biblical conception of the kingdom of God. He never wavered from considering this the central idea of Jesus's gospel, though kings and queens have seldom reigned in the ways the biblical writers understood.

In America, perhaps more than in Britain, the phrase has been deemed unhelpful and at times almost banned because the language, though not the idea behind the language, is no longer regarded as relevant. This criticism raises most sharply the matter of how legitimate it is to use biblical imagery to reach secular society in its doubts and difficulties as, in the West at least, it goes its post-Christian way. But unless, like Paul Tillich, thinkers invent a whole new language for speaking about God, which has then to be learned, what else can Christians do except explain the meaning of biblical ideas while admitting they first developed in an entirely different society?

The same is true of the Sermon on the Mount, that other seminal aspect of Jesus's teaching which first arrested Donald Soper in the early 1930s, if not before, and which some biblical expositors believe was geared to believers alone. Donald considered the injunctions contained there were seminal for all, but did he too often assume people knew the details to which he was referring?

In one sense, though he was aware of the post-Christian nature of Western society, he continued to use biblical ideas, albeit selecting only the few he thought he could explain in an intelligible way. As the following exploration of his theology and spirituality shows, he did have a clearly worked-out Christian view by which he lived and which shaped his responses and interpretations, and it was this view he continually offered as a twentieth-century evangelist.

Clearly he readily equated the coming of the reign of

God with a particular social and political expression rather than understanding faith in a more eschatalogical context, though latterly he laid greater stress on eternity. Moreover, he presented a clearly defined gospel, but perhaps this lacked sufficient subtlety because of his overriding need to reach secular men and women.

The world as the millennium approaches is certainly a different one from that which Donald knew. Perhaps now new and different responses are needed by Christians and others too, but what can be learned by them from Donald's tireless preaching and teaching about God's reign – on TV and radio and in hundreds of other places, most notably, of course, Hyde Park and Tower Hill – is that Christians, whichever century they live in, must put themselves at the centre of conflicts and debates in society and cease to loiter on its periphery.

Donald Soper's twentieth-century pilgrimage (for it was that, as the chronology of his life at the back of this book indicates) is significant because he tried to wrestle with many of the century's main ideas and problems and doubts, as he shared with so many crowds a vision of the truth of Christ which he had seen. 'There is a kingdom of heaven now,' he said to one of those crowds during his month-long visit to Ceylon in 1947, during which he spoke to Buddhists, communists, Christians and those of no faith, including his largest open-air meeting ever of some four thousand on the Galle Face Green in Colombo. 'I have entered it and know what it is. I entered it as I listened to the great music of Kreisler playing the violin at the Guildhall at Cambridge when I was a student. I know what it is to go to heaven by prayer. I personally knew it as a little boy, when at a prayer meeting, a certain old man stood up and prayed. He was an old man, who lived an ordinary life, and could not say two sentences together in conversation without humming and harring, but when he prayed he was transformed and there was eloquence and beauty. I have seen the kingdom of heaven in the minds of little children, in the beauties of Ceylon and in the cathedral at Milan. I have seen it in the goodness of ordinary people.'[57]

Brian Frost
Lent, 1997

Acknowledgments

The publishers and editor gratefully acknowledge the following sources for Lord Soper's comments and reflections:

Sharon Allen Leukaemia Trust; Bellew Publishing; *Big Issue*; Blackwell's (Oxford); BBC – *Any Questions?*, *Everyman*, World Service; the Revd Kenneth Brown; *Care of the Elderly*; Christian Socialist Movement; *Christian World*; Churches Fellowship for Psychical and Spiritual Studies; *Croydon Times*; Epworth Press; Fellowship of Reconciliation; Fulham and Chelsea Adult Education Centre; *Franciscan*; *Hampstead and Highgate Express*; Hansard; Hodder & Stoughton Publishers; Revd George Hunter III; *Illustrated*; ITV; *London Quarterly and Holborn Review*; *Methodist Recorder*; Hayley Mills; Nauman Neame at Take Home Books; *News Chronicle*; the Revd Dr John Newton; Order of Christian Witness; Robson Books; *Spectator*; *Staffordshire Evening Sentinel*; *Sunday Telegraph*; Thames TV; *Tribune*; *Views*; *Yorkshire Post*.

Special thanks are due to Epworth Press for its generosity and to the Revd Philip Spence, who drew the illustrations featured on the cover and in the text.

Prologue: My Testament

I believe in God with my mind because I find it impossible to make sense of the world without there being some guiding principle behind it.[1]

To believe in God is a pilgrimage rather than a proposition.[2]

Our religious experience, though it must include a reasonable approach to faith, is compounded of all kinds of experiences which go far beyond truth – belonging to the realm of love; belonging to the realm of beauty; belonging to the realm of consecrated, dedicated action.[3]

Why do I follow Jesus Christ? Because he has shown me what the love of God can do; and however far I stray from loving my fellow creatures, I know that I belong to them; I know that I am at home with them. Why do I follow Jesus Christ? Because he has shown me the way to interpret this ever more complex and amazing world. He has given me the capacity to fit the various parts of the jigsaw in their places. He has given me a reason for looking forward in hope and a reason for cleansing my own life so that I may express his will.[4]

We have to go many days through desert country, but we should not be unduly concerned if on this journey we have our iron rations with us. They will be sufficient to keep us fit and strong, if only we will partake of them . . . If we fall back on these rations of belief – a belief in God, a confidence in Jesus, and a knowledge of his cross – then I believe we shall have made a beginning that Jesus himself would not despise.[5]

I don't think that religion will be metaphysical, dogmatic, precise, the kind of theology enshrined in what the Christian Church has said. I think we have got to be much more economical with the things we say and much more practical in the things we do.[6]

I was convinced many years ago . . . that religion is essential because we are searchers after something of which we already know the secret in our hearts, but we are never satisfied until we find it. Religion is essential because, although at certain levels we can be indifferent to its claims, when we are faced with the ultimate decision we are helpless and lost without it. And religion is essential because it gives us that coherence and sense of unity. We belong to God; we are children of God. What sort of God? I have found the answer in Jesus Christ. I have found that in him is a God who answers my questions, who stimulates my thoughts, who satisfies my heart, and who leads me into the kingdom. And I have no right to ask more than that. In any case it is sufficient.[7]

The one gospel that no one could ignore would be the good news of a world society making and keeping the peace and justice for everybody. But then I believe that is the one and original gospel.[8]

This widespread assumption that a religious creed is super-fluous in the twentieth century as the basis upon which adequate human relationships are to be built will not bear analysis.[9]

I want people to use religion not as an escape from an intolerable world but a gateway into a better one.[10]

I am a pacifist revolutionary.[11]

I simply want to be remembered for what I am – one of John Wesley's travelling preachers.[12]

My entire being – spiritual, moral, political, philosophical – is composed of one assurance. There is nothing wrong with God. The trouble is with his family.[13]

What I Live For

The best short answer for a Christian minister is 'I live to love God and enjoy him for ever.' That is the strategy of the good life for me – its tactics are to seek the kingdom of God as Jesus bids us do.

However, these words are no more intelligible and meaningful than a code message. Let me try to break the code.

I live for the day when all God's children will have enough to eat . . .

I live for the day when the Christmas proclamation of 'Peace on Earth' will come true . . .

I live for world government – I don't believe that the nation state is part of God's kingdom at all . . . Only a world government can give black and brown and yellow men and women an equal place in this world with white people – and

I live for that day because God is the Father of us all and has no favourites among his children.

Of course I believe that people need forgiveness and the grace of God. But I know of no better way of preparing for the first and enjoying the second than what I have been saying.

I should be a humbug unless I made it clear that by myself I couldn't live for any of these things – only when God in his mercy lives in me can I begin to live for him.[14]

I believe in a Church which in obedience to Jesus Christ will declare the gospel of non-violent love in personal relationships and throughout the entire realm of industrial and international affairs, but that is a revolutionary and most dangerous enterprise which can only be undertaken in a spirit of utter faith in a God to whom we are driven by the sense of our tremendous need.[15]

I am more certain than ever that [our] twentieth-century problems will send us back, if we are wise, 1,900 years to the Sermon on the Mount and the Man on the Cross. It is the light that streams both from the Mount and the Cross and the pentecostal experience that it illuminates by which we must find the answer.[16]

The Christian Faith

Donald Soper was aware of both God's awesomeness and his approachability. For him God was marked too by friendliness and had characteristics which were at least describable as personal. Necessary to this belief was his central conviction that God had become human in Jesus, who had revealed a God of love rather than one of power, a God of service rather than one of miracle.

Donald was gripped again and again by the Christmas story with its promise of peace on earth for people of goodwill. Here he was more Catholic than Protestant in his emphasis; but in his awareness of the humanity rather than the divinity of Jesus he was more a liberal Protestant. Supremely Donald was arrested by the struggles, conflicts and relationships Jesus forged with his disciples and friends, and what he termed Jesus's 'moral excellence'.

He was not unaware of Jesus's sublimity, of course, but, unusually for a Christian minister, saw Jesus making compromises, concerned more for ethics than eschatology, who lived out and was prepared to die for a non-violent way of life.

Donald brooded too on the mystery of suffering and could only conclude that, although there was no easy answer to it, many who had suffered greatly still believed. Indeed, there was a residue of suffering which seemed to be at the heart of God's purpose. There was also a perpetual struggle against sin, both personal and corporate, which Christ's life and, supremely, death had dealt with finally.

Jesus, Donald was convinced, had identified God with the human condition, and the love which he had disclosed would overcome the evils of the world. In one sense for him Jesus was always the elder brother who went ahead of men and women, showing the way. Yet he was also the child of Bethlehem, destined to become the man who reigned from the cross and the 'king of all creation'. From that cross he demonstrated that all human beings were sisters and brothers of one human family. Hence for Donald Christianity had a universal quality which went way beyond the boundaries of the Church and included all peoples and their histories.

Jesus's love drew deep responses from Donald Soper and made him want to follow that revolutionary path as well as celebrate Jesus's resurrection, which for him was the guarantee of Christian faith and life and the beginning of Jesus's ministry across the centuries through the Church. For him the Church was always central, with a vital part to play in transforming history because the Holy Spirit had given power to all disciples to enable them to love and embrace the Christian life with both courage and joy.

Christians were also to be co-creators with God through the Holy Spirit, who enabled Jesus, by Bible study and worship, especially the Eucharist, to become our contemporary. Through Christ's Church the world itself could be revolutionised in all its facets as the Body of Christ set about becoming light and salt for broken humanity.

Christianity is . . .

The predominant characteristic of Christianity is that you do things differently and you do different things.[1]

Christianity is an announcement rather than an argument about God.[2]

Christianity is first a great declaration about God . . . but it is also just as great a declaration about men and women.[3]

Christianity is not something you can achieve. It is not good advice. It is good news.[4]

Christianity was intended to be a lantern a well as a searchlight.[5]

The apocalyptic concept that has often been found in Christian thinking is the only true concept which is appropriate for us today.[6]

The distinguishing mark of Christianity is neither its private piety, nor its metaphysic, but its practical expression in Jesus of the 'way of love' and the 'way of life'.[7]

One of the outstanding characteristics of Christianity is that it is an Order of Service.[8]

That which distinguishes and identifies the Christian faith is non-violence.[9]

Christianity is a way of life, not a way of looking at life.[10]

Christianity is about the kingdom of God and how to get there, rather than about our souls and how to feed them.[11]

Christianity is ninety-nine per cent obedience.[12]

Christianity is profoundly controversial because it is profound.[13]

Christianity is revolutionary.[14]

Christianity is contagious; you catch it rather than achieve it.[15]

Christianity is narrow-minded in the sense that its mind is set on the 'narrow way' which Jesus said leads to life rather than the 'broad way' that he said leads to destruction.[16]

The paradox at the heart of Christianity is that what we regard as the weak virtues are actually the strong ones.[17]

Christianity is good news for today. It interprets the past and opens up the future because it changes the present.[18]

The Christian faith is the promise of God through Jesus Christ that we shall find our happiness and our leisure as the by-product of our attention to those things that belong to his kingdom.[19]

Christianity is self-development, not self-expression.[20]

Christianity is something for sinners and not for saints. And the saints are those who, having started as sinners, become more and more like the saints.[21]

God

God: perfect one and perfect society.
Mystery and awe: but also Father and Friend.[1]

The essence of the doctrine of the Trinity is that I as a person depend on outside commitments and outside relations in order to be a person.[2]

I must think of God as personal – at least as personal as the human creature who can think about him. Otherwise, the part would be greater than the whole, the painting would be superior to the artist.[3]

I cannot explain God. It's like a man who's blind trying to describe the sunshine.[4]

God is revealed in the universe which he has created as the poet is revealed in the sonnet which he has composed.[5]

God is the supreme artist rather than the supreme scientist.[6]

God, the mysterious, the wonderful, the aweful, the beckoning, the loving creator, is the ultimate ground of all reality and especially of what we call the realm of moral values.[7]

In many respects I'm a pantheist.[8]

I believe God is the inward reality. I do not believe God is 'out there'.[9]

God is on the movement side of creation.[10]

God is the ongoing cause of change.[11]

———•———

It is most dangerous to regard God as the one who fills out the gaps because the gaps tend to narrow.[12]

Unless there is a God no one would want to find him.[13]

The only God worth believing in is the God of truth.[14]

The God in whom I believe is as much interested in human laughter as in human progress.[15]

A great deal of the power of God is in our hands.[16]

———•———

The gospel is the good news of what God has done, is doing and will do. This is revealed in Jesus Christ, who is the perfect revelation of God and whose cross is the instrument of salvation.[17]

Unless we guard this vital element of a divine 'self-emptying', the entire fabric of human life falls to pieces: good, evil, reward and punishment, responsibility and effort become meaningless, and we are nothing more than puppets dangled and jerked upon a cardboard stage. Such is the irreversible logic of divine omnipotence when it is divorced from divine purpose. What seems to me to be the Christian message is that, by the grace of God, we do possess his power to overcome the wars and hatreds and evils which afflict us. We are partners with him in true omnipotence; that is the fact of the gospel – the good news which I would like you all to hear and to believe.[18]

You don't find God by looking into the heavens: you find God by looking into a crib.[19]

The universe is on the side of righteousness and peace – for God is at work for us and with us. The Christmas message is the one authentic hope for the future.[20]

The Sermon on the Mount is a description of what happens if you obey God today; and if you obey God today, it is God who, in the Christian view, largely takes charge of tomorrow.[21]

You can't have the brotherhood of man without the fatherhood of God. You need theology before you can have social justice.[22]

I have never been able to explain the existence of evil . . . I don't know how to reconcile evil in the world and the love of God. I only know some of the greatest sufferers have been the greatest believers.[23]

Within the framework of the fatherhood of God, whose purpose is the creation of a family and ultimate spiritual union with himself, this world as a vale of soul-making, the presence of evil as the price of freedom that God's children must be able to exercise if we are to grow, the notion of one increasing purpose and the concept of eternal life all begin to cohere in one pattern.[24]

There is a residue of suffering which is the very heart of God's purpose, and therefore cannot be evil in origin. It is rather part of the raw material out of which God intends to grow our souls.[25]

. . . the permission of evil in the world by God is a necessary counterpart to his desire for good, for if you had no chance to go wrong, there is no possible virtue in going right.[26]

There is in pain such a peculiarly personal element that it is dangerous to try to measure it. In one real sense, there is no more pain in the whole world than the pain of one individual suffering pain. You can't add up pain. And because this question is so intensely personal, it cannot be treated in a scientific and public way.[27]

I should regard it as impossible to reconcile the love of God with the fact of suffering if the grave were the end . . . I think now, that if this world were all, then what I saw at Auschwitz would for ever prevent me from believing in a God who was anything like a human parent and who had anything like love as his chief characteristic.[28]

I have never doubted original sin. I find it a continuous menace, and I accept it. I don't accept it in the sense that I can do nothing about it.[29]
Sin is the second strongest thing in the universe.[30]

The doctrine of the Holy Spirit is the truth that in the realm of moral values, of prayer and meditation, of worship and praise, of sacrament and mysticism – God in nature – in every person and uniquely in Jesus, God comes into our lives to enable us to solve our questions and dilemmas. Thus he has come to us in natural beauty, in the orderliness of the physical world, in the inspired masterpieces of the artists, in the religious genius of the Buddha and in the mystical experiences of a Catherine of Compostella ... When we speak of Jesus as Lord, we assert his uniqueness and perfection in a spiritual sphere in which many others have proved their claim to be regarded as masters and teachers.[31]

I use the word Holy Spirit to describe the highest of our capacities to understand and to be, as consequent upon the all-pervasive purposes and idea of God.[32]

For practical purposes the Holy Spirit is the spirit of Jesus.[33]

Incarnation

... the birth of Jesus links yesterday, today and tomorrow together in the eternal plan of God.[1]

Christmas contains the microcosm of all the main characteristics of the kingdom of God.[2]

Peace on earth rests in the promise of Christmas.[3]

Jesus is the symbol of God's goodwill to us – therefore it is worth while expressing goodwill to one another. The baby born of a peasant mother in a cow shed is nevertheless the Son of God and therefore we can be sure of the true status of every human being and particularly of the poor and oppressed. The Christmas story is the sufficient ground for our confidence that peace, security, justice, love and eternity beckon to the real world and are worthy of looking for and striving for because they can be attained.[4]

The fact that Jesus was humbly born and not miraculously set down on this earth, the fact that his revelation of the love of God was not made in some metaphysical demonstration of the Divine Power but in his perfect obedience to his heavenly Father, the fact that he was fully human and was tempted like we are – these are the basic data that are enshrined in the Christmas message. These truths must rigorously be distinguished from all other devotional, mystical, imaginative, poetic things which have quite properly gathered round them and invested them with beauty and with all embellishments that the creative spirit of men and women can bring to them . . .[5]

When the magical and the primitive elements have been stripped away from the Christmas story it is to me the most realistic presentation in a historic setting of the eternal problem of good and evil . . . It epitomises the struggle for peace in the middle of tyranny and for justice and well-being in a world of privilege. For the first time in history the claim is made that a little child is the 'rightful King of all creation', and unless we become as little children we shall not even see into the kingdom of God.[6]

Christmas is the hope of the world because its message of peace and goodwill is not just a beautiful but impractical dream. Here in Bethlehem is the real world and we are only living when we believe it and are prepared to act upon that belief.[7]

Those who keep Christmas are making, however brief, a pilgrimage to another source of power – the power of love set in the halo of family life, the power of the responsible society, where every human being is the brother or sister of the Holy Child of Bethlehem.[8]

To visit a stable at Bethlehem and to think of a helpless baby, who grew into a gentle man and died in loyalty to a creed of non-violent love, is to catch sight of another kind of power which is evidence both of a good world and of a reasonable one as well.[9]

If the lights of Christmas were on all the time, what a different world it would be. But Christ's life – and death and resurrection – has overcome the darkness of mind and spirit. And through Jesus, our elder brother . . . the night is passed.[10]

Jesus Christ

Jesus, the Son of Man

Jesus is the incarnation and fulfilment of God's purpose.[1]

It still remains true, if we begin with Jesus as the friend of sinners, as our friend, we then by that process end up not with the human Jesus but with the Jesus whom we call Lord and Master.[2]

Jesus Christ is pre-eminent . . . because of his special and unique quality that he calls love; because of the unique and special thing he calls peace – the peace which passes understanding; because of the peculiar and especial quality which he calls joy . . .

Joy is the inner sense of victory, an inner sense of triumph. It was something Jesus had, so that the defection of his friends, the hostility of the crowd and the arduousness of his way left him untouched. It is a quality of serenity.[3]

The divinity and saviourhood of the Master lose nothing of their vitality because they are found alongside human frailty and human limitation. For me, at least, they could have no other context.[4]

There is a moral excellence and eminence in Jesus.[5]

The Christian gospel, as laid down and lived out by Jesus Christ, was a revolutionary one for the individual and society. It involved a new attitude to neighbourliness, to violence, to economics and to politics. It demanded, in fact, a new social order to house the new spirit . . .[6]

Jesus is the greatest practical revolutionary the world has ever known because he saw so plainly that thinking and action must always go hand in hand.[7]

Jesus in Galilee

It is impossible to talk about Jesus without seeing the emphasis he laid on those who are denied the opportunities of life.[8]

Jesus himself proclaimed again and again that the nature of goodness is always personal. Moreover, there is irrefutable evidence that Jesus led his disciples step by step towards larger and larger objectives, many of which, at a particular point of time, were out of reach.[9]

When Jesus lived in Palestine, the love and power of God were expressed through his human body, in the eyes that smiled, in the hand that touched the cripple . . .[10]

The amazing thing about Jesus is that when he had the whole world to win, he wasted time, as it were, in talking to Mary, to Martha, to the woman at the well, to Zaccheus and to Nicodemus, because Jesus knew that the whole meaning of love is personal or it is nothing . . .[11]

Jesus transfigured the ordinary events of life with an inner meaning through parables.[12]

. . . the same Master who said, 'Take my yoke upon you, for I am meek and humble of heart,' also thundered against all-powerful Pharisees, withered their complacency under his condemnation, swept the money-changers out of the Temple by the dynamic authority of his moral purity (not, let me add, by the physical compulsion of the whip) and cowed Pilate with his sublime courage.[13]

Jesus, in the Sermon on the Mount, reconciles the two great fields of human experience. First, the world of hard material facts, the realm of circumstance and economics, with their vital effects upon every part of our life; second, the world of aspiration and hope, the realm of art and vision, without which the world would be an empty place even for the materialist.[14]

Jesus Christ, in his earthly ministry, was involved in compromise. He could not have preached at all had he not been prepared to do so within the protection of the very Roman Empire which his kingdom was to overthrow.[15]

. . . the Gospels do clearly demonstrate the truth that our blessed Lord himself was only able to exhibit his perfect sinlessness in the interior world of unswerving loyalty to his Father. He perfectly *intended* to do the will of his heavenly Father. Yet his actions, however sublime in intention, were morally imperfect in that they were within a framework of possible options, none of which was wide enough to permit of the full exercise of that perfect will . . .[16]

In the strictest meaning of the word 'compromise', let us face the fact that our blessed Lord was driven to compromise himself. He did not provoke a quarrel with the authorities. He was prepared to *give* his life; but only when the giving was of the uttermost significance. It is hinted at – sometimes it is plainly stated – that he avoided conflict because he was not ready. He was not prepared to be trapped, and on one occasion when people were desperately concerned to know what their duty was, he threw their problem back at them: 'Render unto Caesar the things that are Caesar's, and render unto God the things that are God's.' He accepted the indirect protection of Roman soldiers. He complimented and befriended a centurion. He ate the meals of those who exploited their fellows . . .[17]

What Jesus is saying – and his life and death and rising again is an exemplification of the truth – is that love goes beyond what can be regarded as justice.[18]

The Christian ethic, for Jesus, began in objectives. Jesus said, 'Seek ye first *the kingdom of God*.' That is the expression in all his teachings in the Sermon on the Mount. For Jesus, ethics were bound up in the search for the kingdom of God, which is a way of life which God will have his children live.[19]

Christianity would never have been on this planet if Jesus had taken the sword.[20]

Jesus combined the realism of a gradual exposition of the good life throughout the years of his ministry with the perfect witness to that good life at his Passion.[21]

Jesus was not a passive instrument of prophecy. He was the supreme strategist who grasped the broad outline of God's plan for him. He was the supreme tactician who worked out the plan in detail. In these, as in so many other matters, our Lord was master of insight rather than foresight.[22]

Jesus in Jerusalem

Watching Jesus going to his death has taught me the marvellous economy of our Lord's character. He had no pre-occupation with either living or dying. His whole mind was set to fulfil his vocation.[23]

. . . on that first Passion Sunday Jesus set his face to go to Jerusalem – he took the great decision which led inexorably to his arrest, and trial, and death, and rising again.

In one sense our Lord had taken that decision years ago when, as a boy of twelve in the Temple, he had warned his mother who had been searching for him, 'Did you not know that I must be about my Father's business?' It was the same decision that he made again when he came to John in the wilderness to be baptised and dedicated himself to his ministry of preaching and healing . . . But in a special sense the decision which Jesus took on this day was the most vital and important of all, for his choice was literally a matter of life and death. He had come, as the hymn says, 'with all his grace to save a fallen race'. He had already given people the truth that was in him. He had given them the love that was in him, and now he sets out for Jerusalem to give them his life itself. He knows that he will be killed yet he has made up his mind even to die in agony on a cross so that his fellow creatures may find their way to God's kingdom.[24]

I think of Jesus starting out on that last journey with all its pain and sorrow. I think that perhaps the hardest thing that he had to bear was the terrible fact that he knew he would be alone . . .[25]

Love is goodwill on fire. It is the persistent care of others. In fact, it is the way Jesus lived and died. He loved his disciples; he loved the crowds when they acclaimed him. He went on loving them when they forsook him. He loved his disciples when they professed their ardent determination to follow him to death and beyond. He went on loving them when one of them betrayed him, another denied him and the rest ran away. That's love – indefatigable goodwill.[26]

Jesus on the Cross

Jesus was crucified because he preached a hard and subversive gospel . . . in which the 'meek would inherit the earth' and a worldwide realm of peace and goodwill would come into being . . .[27]

When he died on the cross, he died for the people of God: for people like Peter and James, people like Mary Magdalene, people like Martha and Mary, people like the

Pharisees and Sadducees, and the ordinary fishermen and tax-gatherers.[28]

We are all brothers and sisters for whom Christ died.[29]

Jesus prayed the perfect prayer . . . 'If it be possible, let this cup [the suffering and shame of the cross] pass from me: nevertheless not as I will, but as thou wilt . . .[30]

The cross was the final expression of Jesus's commitment to love of neighbour and enemy.[31]

Jesus was crucified because he was a political revolutionary.[32]

The impact of Jesus was to foment and create a communist society.[33]

Jesus not only epitomises the struggle between good and evil in the souls of men and women, but in the events that cluster around his death are all the factors that accompany this struggle in the organised life of society as well.[34]

Jesus went to his cross to prove the value and ultimate victory of non-violent love.[35]

His dying was the divine gesture of suffering love untainted by the smallest ingredient of violence in thought and word and deed.[36]

Jesus showed us that the way of suffering . . . can be a divine energy whereby that which resists all other kinds of authority and power can be overcome.[37]

Jesus did not wait for people to repent. He died for them while
they were yet sinners: would there have been a Christian faith
had it been otherwise?[38]

Jesus died in absolute confidence that God is good. If you
believe that, beyond all the pain there is peace.[39]

The last and most important word from Jesus on his cross is
that we commend ourselves to God in hope, in the kind of
faith which is much more trust than certainty and in the kind
of love which we can catch almost as an infection from those
we know . . . who are representative of that love [which] shines
out of them.[40]

For all who thirst let them come to the waters, the waters
of love and of sorrow – the tears of Mary and the comfort
of Jesus as he remembers and expresses, for us and for all,
that God is our Father and we are his children. We belong
together in that integument of love and responsibility. By his
grace we can indeed establish that which has never yet been
fulfilled, the family life in which all are cared for and none
left out. These are some of the ripples, the shock waves, of
these memorable words of Jesus, 'Woman, behold thy son! . . .
Behold thy mother!'[41]

The Risen Christ

Easter is the festival of hope.[42]

Supremely at Easter Christians have something to shout about,
the tremendous fact, the all-important fact of history, that once

upon a time Jesus Christ, the man approved by God, as Peter said, was cruelly and infamously put to death. He was buried and on the third day he rose from the grave. He came back to his friends – he actually came back to convince Mary in the garden, and his disciples in the upper room and on the road to Emmaus and by the shore, that he was in fact all that he claimed to be, to prove that his extraordinary, amazing gospel was true.[43]

I believe in the resurrection because it is authenticated by the facts.[44]

The first Easter is the vindication of the spiritual world for all who will make their pilgrimage to the garden tomb. As Christians we say that the world can be saved even at this eleventh hour of its folly, just as we say that penitent sinners can be saved in their last earthly moments. Our confidence for such an amazing claim is the spiritual graces which flow to poor sinners' hearts when they cast themselves upon the mercy of God. Similarly, we are bold to claim that spiritual powers will be let loose into our corporate affairs at the point of our sufficient trust in God's will and way.[45]

If there were no Easter in human experience, there would be no God such as Jesus taught and loved. Jesus would have been mistaken and his teaching an impossible dream. It is because Jesus conquered death that we are made sure of the God he made manifest and, with God, are confident that all these things are possible.[46]

The resurrection was the establishment of the continuing ministry of Jesus.[47]

Jesus has returned and does return – as in Francis of Assisi and also through humble people who are the expression of the spirit of Jesus.[48]

The Pentecostal Community

The Power of Pentecost

Let not your heart be troubled; you believe in God. Believe also in Jesus Christ: stand firm. Love the brethren and look for Pentecost, and my friends, I believe you will find it . . .[1]

Pentecost, as the crowning gift of God, is also the complete and satisfying answer to every problem and sorrow which vexes us all. If I could communicate nothing else . . . I would pass on to you that certainty . . . that our salvation is in him who first taught us how to live, then showed us how to die, then came back to us to make his promise good and finally bestowed upon us the gift of his Holy Spirit.[2]

I find perhaps the greatest comfort and strength, on the day called Whit Sunday, in the certainty that this is a miraculous world. I believe in miracles; I have seen them too often to doubt them. Here was a miracle, a miracle of grace and power, which came into the lives of men and women who were waiting to receive some new gift, and out of it new miracles happened . . .[3]

Pentecost celebrates the birthday of the Church and announces the power to put the world right.[4]

Power comes to those who obey God – not only power to tell the truth and to keep pure and to be unselfish, but also power to change the moral climate of the world, to win all kinds of people to faith and hope, to make peace between the nations and to create a family life everywhere.[5]

By the grace of God we are not puppets dangled on a string – we are live, real human beings and in our hands is the destiny of the world, in so far as our temporal affairs are concerned. Over and above all is the unchanging and everlasting God: within, penetrating it, is the Holy Spirit. But in the framework of that vast scheme of things which we call the Christian purpose and plan, you and I are the arbiters of our own fate.[6]

We who celebrate God's Holy Spirit believe that has a great deal to do with common sense fortified by erudition and carried out in politics and economics.[7]

The Church and Its Worship

The first Christians knew exactly where they were going – they were going into a new kind of human relationship and they had turned their back on the establishment. They were therefore baptised – the symbol of the complete break with the past.

They held themselves entirely responsible for their mutual welfare – the physical necessaries constituted a right to be enjoyed by everyone, irrespective of moral worth. So 'they broke bread together.' Finally they recognised that the cult of private property was the supreme enemy of the good society, so they 'held things in common' and practised the 'commonwealth'. And it worked till there were too many Ananiases and not enough Stephens; then it broke down and gave way to the 'Holy' Roman Empire. The story of the first Christian Church contains both that promise and that warning.[8]

The resurrected Christ is not confined to a time or a place nor available as he was in Galilee. His continuing presence and power is available in the Church, which is his body. Outside the Church there is no salvation.[9]

The Church must recover its sense of wonder.[10]

If you have heard the voice of God in the message of the Cross; if you have been stirred as you cried out on Easter Sunday, 'He is risen indeed,' if you have been impressed by the inevitable fact of the gift of the Holy Spirit and if you have been persuaded on Trinity Sunday to take your shoes off and recognise that there are far more things in this world than can be extrapolated ... I believe, in that kind of experience, having heard God speak, you can abide his silence.[11]

I believe that the only true and certain road to human happiness is the road of prayer, penitence and worship.[12]

A faith which is unscaffolded by the sacramental and liturgical content is incomplete and inadequate. It is in disciplined worship, both in our individual devotion and in our corporate fellowship, that we begin to know the mysteries of the common life in the body of Christ.[13]

I have found the service of Holy Communion something that is . . . mine to cherish . . . [something by] which we can be nourished and build up one another.[14]

Here, in one brief act, is all Christianity in essence, all earth and heaven, the centre and soul of all faith.[15]

In whatever form the Communion Service is set forth, and whatever may be the particular significance we attach to it – either recollection, or remembrance, or sacrifice, or sacrament – these things, although they are important, are not finally decisive. What is decisive is that when those to whom we appeal have come to the point at which they can make a total response, then that total response should be made within the framework, the pattern, the ideology, the mysticism, the meaning, all of the imagery of the self-giving of Christ, the offering of Christ, the *Totus Christus*.[16]

I do not take the bread and wine expecting that as I rise from my knees I shall either see a bright light that will dispel my doubts and fears or feel a sense of goodness in my heart. I think of Jesus; I see him in the bread and wine; I confide in his offer; and I ask that nothing in me may impede the flow of his goodness. I leave the rest to him . . .[17]

When I stretch out my hands to receive the bread and when I lift it up to my lips I testify to the life which goes beyond the world of sense and time – that world where alone is peace and justice and love.[18]

It is very difficult to get to know Jesus merely by reading in the Gospels; but let me test the Gospels by those who've been

the saints and, supremely, let me believe, through the wine
and spiritual nutriment that comes with the bread, that this
eucharistic feast is the time-honoured way in which, in spirit,
we can come near to Christ.[19]

The Bible

The Bible is the Word which is in the words.[20]

You should read the Bible starting at the fifth chapter of
Matthew and not the first chapter of Genesis.[21]

Read the Ten Commandments as the first lesson on Sunday
morning and the Sermon on the Mount as the second
lesson.[22]

To be educated by the Bible we must read it and not gather
snippets from it here and there . . . we must read it with our
minds open, and apply to what we read all the imagination
and criticism and sensitivity we can bring . . . we must read it
as if we were looking over the shoulder of Jesus, and he is telling
us where to begin and how to understand what to believe.[23]

When we see Jesus we see the truth, for all the other stories
of the Bible become true in the story of Jesus. There is the
story of truth; there is life as it most really exists.[24]

The Bible says what you want it to if you look up the
appropriate text.[25]

The Bible is the most dangerous totalitarian instrument, though
it is an infinitely valuable document.[26]

The Bible is a marvellous servant but an intolerable master.[27]

The Bible isn't a book. It's a library.[28]

All that can be understood and gathered from this book is summed up, consummated, in Jesus Christ, whom we find in Bethlehem, in Nazareth, in Galilee, in Jerusalem, on the cross, by the empty tomb, and then among his friends again. That is what the Bible means. It means that our lives become intelligible and real when we know Jesus Christ.[29]

The People of God

The body of Jesus was the solitary witness on the cross to the Will of God, so that the Body of Christ could become the instrument of that will today.[30]

The truth of the Christian faith is not that you are children to be rescued but that you are co-partners with God to rescue others. It is God who calls us to the work begun in his creation and continued in Jesus and his cross – a work to be continued and ended only when we all give our allegiance to him . . . If the Christian people of this land would give themselves to the belief that they are the loved children of God, and then would walk out fearlessly to do his holy will, I believe that the greatest miracle of the ages would happen and that the power of God would come upon this poor, broken earth . . .[31]

God is waiting to give peace and goodwill to his world because it is his family and he loves every child in it. He is the heavenly Father who does not demand that we should all be morally excellent before we secure his bounties but only that we should take our places around his table in the confidence that he will be there at its head to make the family complete.[32]

The Church of Christ, as I understand it, is commissioned by its Lord to challenge not only the sins of the individual but the whole world order, economic and political, which stands between us and the realisation of the kingdom, to attack everything which checks the soul's spiritual energy. It is to be the leaven which revolutionises the lump.[33]

The Church has too often set its target too low – has so frequently applauded itself for its minor achievements. We are the body of Christ – to be salt and light of the world.[34]

The Church is the body of Christ – Christ's hands, feet, smiles, words. *We* are the Church.[35]

We who make up this Christian Church must be the hands and feet and smile and even the wounds of Jesus, so that when people see what we do with our hands it may remind them of Jesus, and when they see the errands on which our feet go, and the look on our faces, and even the way we bear our sorrows and our suffering, they may remember his love. But just as our arms and legs only work properly when they obey the directions we give them from our head, so we cannot be his hands and feet unless we are formed together as a body is, each one of us obeying him as our head.[36]

Christian revolutionaries begin by creating inside the system which they are concerned to overthrow groups or cells of people who, with the limited freedom they possess, create centres of new life, practise as far as they are able the techniques of that new life; and by the multiplication of these cells a revolutionary change begins to take place in which they live. There is unmistakable evidence in the Gospels that this was the initial method employed by Jesus to publicise his gospel and to prosecute his aims.[37]

Whatever I do, I am bearing in my body his marks, and, whatever I do, may they see my good works and glorify, through me, him who is my Father. That is a high calling, but it is the calling of the servant . . .[38]

Soper's Soapbox 1

Reporter: (*on Dr Soper's arrival in New York*) Is God dead?
Dr Soper: (*knowing there was a theological school claiming precisely that*) I hadn't heard that God was unwell.

Dr Soper: Talking about Christianity without saying anything about sin is rather like discussing gardening without saying anything about weeds.
(*Practical Christianity Today*, p. 26)

Dr Soper: (*to crowd*) Think what God does to a garden when left to himself.
(Hyde Park, 11 November 1984)

Questioner: What do you think of born-again Christians?

Dr Soper: In many respects I liked them better before it happened. I would infinitely rather have a born-again communist than a born-again Christian . . .

(Hyde Park, 11 November 1984)

———•———

Questioner: If you were made redundant, what would your attitude be to accepting the dole?

Dr Soper: With sin running at its present rate, we are not going to become redundant.

(*Any Questions?*, April 1982)

Questioner: What would you do to cure it?

Dr Soper: What would I do to cure what?

Questioner: Powellism.

Dr Soper: Our friend is asking, 'How do you deal with sin?' (*Laughter.*) That, of course, is the ultimate question. I'm very glad you asked about it. (*Chuckles from crowd.*) It's up my alley, if I may say so. (*Convulsive laughter.*) It's not so easy; let's start there. I've been at it for some years, and there's still a fair amount of it going round. Mind you, it's my stock in trade, so I don't want to exhaust it before I retire.

(Quoted in George Hunter III, *Evangelical Rhetoric in Secular Britain: The Theory and Speaking of Donald Soper and Bryan Green*, unpublished thesis, Evanston, Illinois, 1972, p. 401)

Heckler: You use the word wickedness . . .

Dr Soper: Yes, I use the word wickedness. Quite often I do.

You'd be surprised how many of my sermons at any rate begin there ... There isn't a state in the world that isn't wicked. There isn't a single one in this crowd who isn't wicked. I'm trying not to look particularly in certain directions.

Heckler: You speak for yourself.

Dr Soper: He is the only holy person in a crowd composed of several sinners. You wouldn't agree that you're perfect, would you?

Heckler: No.

Dr Soper: Having settled that theological point, let's get on with the inference ...

(Hyde Park, 3 April 1983)

———◆———

Questioner: How would you like to spend your last day on earth?

Dr Soper: By making arrangements for my trip to the other world. This world is an anteroom to a world which is ampler and wider.

(*Any Questions?*, 2 April 1976)

Questioner: What proof do you have of an afterlife?

Dr Soper: Of course I haven't any proof of anything. I haven't even any proof that you're there or all there! But I assume it.

(Hyde Park, 5 November 1978)

———◆———

Dr Soper: If you make a fuss, you get things done.

Questioner: Do I take it you speak for the Church militant?

Dr Soper: The Church triumphant, I hope!

(*Any Questions?*, 23 September 1960)

The Christian Way

Donald Soper's journey of faith across so many decades focused on being both a pilgrim and a disciple. There was about his pilgrimage a restless searching and probing. For him there was no settled place but rather a continuing exploration which was both dynamic and never-ending.

Jesus called disciples, made and shaped them, and those who followed long enough and dug deeply enough discovered that they were intended to journey the way of the cross, as Jesus himself had.

In being obedient to their calling, Christians learned both to respond to God's love and to grow in love for others, including their enemies. Such discipleship, Donald was convinced, led Christians into the public arena, where they were asked to live out the injunctions of the Beatitudes.

On their journey of faith Christians had to be acutely aware of their need to be identified with God's will through prayer, which, because it belonged to the real world, could change individuals and society too if enough people prayed fervently. For Donald, therefore, prayer was practical rather than mystical, prophetic more than priestly, though he was not unaware there were other areas both to discover and to develop.

Another aspect of Donald Soper's journey was the search for holiness. He earnestly sought to be abandoned to God, not only in prayer and worship but also through growth in

Christian maturity, which involved greater awareness of God and openness to the world's sorrows and pains.

Goodness for Donald was no soft option; rather it was the prerequisite for action. So when he talked about being a revolutionary it was always in the context of his conviction that what was required was a moral revolution which involved persistent goodwill towards others.

One overarching theme possessed Donald in all his strivings – the biblical idea of the kingdom, the reign of God over all life, which Christians were committed to proclaim. It was an idea which he expounded in season and out of season, whose focus he found in the Sermon on the Mount. He linked his belief in the kingdom to community – the family life of the entire world, for brotherhood and sisterhood were rooted for him in his belief that God was the Creator of all. The kingdom was not the Church, but the Church existed to point to, bear witness to, and join with others in seeking, that life for all which was God's gift and something human beings had to strive to accomplish, as the Lord's Prayer itself indicated.

Forgiveness was another great theme which dominated Donald's preaching and teaching. It informed much of his work and approach to both personal and political life. It sprang partly from his deep conviction of the fallibility of life on earth and of what human beings do to each other. It sprang too from his knowledge of himself, as he realised he was not only a pilgrim but a penitent one. There were thus two foci for him – repentance and confession on the one hand, forgiveness and a new start on the other.

He struggled often for faith, for he could easily have been an agnostic. He struggled equally to grow in love, for he knew incorrigible egoism often got in the way of what God willed to do with and through Christians.

Increasingly, therefore, he came to emphasise the importance of hope – a virtue he considered was often despised or neglected and relegated to a minor role in Christian life. For Donald, indeed, hope was the ingredient which kept him going, the virtue he could espouse when the other two were unattainable and so latterly he came to speak of it with increasing warmth and respect.

Pilgrimage and Discipleship

Pilgrimage

What I admire about Jesus is that he doesn't ask for my pity or my sorrow. He asks that I should follow him whatever the cost . . .[1]

No people can be seized of the sublime truths of the crucifixion unless in thought and in feeling they take their place at the foot of the cross – but only pilgrims can come to that cross. You can't make an excursion to Calvary – and a pilgrimage is a long and serious journey that starts way back and takes time and patience and perseverance – but the joy and understanding of pilgrims, when at long last they kneel to worship the God they have travelled so far to find, is infinitely worth while.[2]

I'm a pilgrim on a road rather than a prospector with a map, and the best guidance on that road is goodness.[3]

We are on a pilgrimage, and that pilgrimage is never satisfied until we have gone beyond the horizon which now is the furthest point of our vision.[4]

. . . that which we want to see at the end of the road we must envisage clearly in project and purpose as we continue our journey.[5]

The kingdom and the Communion table may seem like 'iron rations' for the Christian pilgrims of this modern age, but they will prove sufficient for the present stage of the journey.[6]

The real essence of the Christian life is not in success but in faithfulness.[7]

We are called to be the pioneers, blazing the trail into the kind of world into which we hope all nations will come.[8]

As a pilgrim I am the more certain than I ever was of a reasonable, justifiable and final end to pilgrimage on this planet.[9]

I yearn for a return to the kind of Christianity which is, first of all, a searching of our hearts that we may discover his new way of life; a Christianity which today would set out to translate the words of Jesus for this twentieth century, so that we could see the footmarks of the Master along the streets of London and Moscow, Peking and New York – and, walking in those footmarks, could be content with the iron rations of adventure.[10]

The end of the road is the enjoyment of God.[11]

Discipleship

The most important part of the Christian faith is discipleship.[12]

I have no use for those who have got their spiritual hats and coats on, waiting for the next world, when they should be rolling up their sleeves in this.[13]

It is my belief that, when people welcome Jesus into the rooms of their minds, into the rooms of their hearts and into the rooms of their wills, he comes in not trailing clouds of theology and glory but as he once did to fishermen and tax-gatherers, as he did to the woman at the well.[14]

There is quite enough which is unequivocal and unmistakable in what Jesus has to say to anyone who will take the first step of repentance and faith. Why not get on with that and leave the rest to be discovered on the march?[15]

The temptations which came to Jesus were the result of the call which he received and the mission which he intended to pursue . . . Our temptations come from the desires of our own hearts and the intentions of our own minds, and the temptations which afflict us have a correspondence in the nature of our commitment, or lack of it . . . I believe grace is available for those who, like Jesus, recognise the nature of the temptations which would have frustrated his ministry, resist those temptations and find comfort and assurance in the grace of God to overcome them . . .[16]

My business is not with Christian perfection as the entire absence of any roots of sin; it is with perfect love as the excellence of the God-filled life. Jesus is my great example.[17]

We love him, because he first loved us. We love him not for some shoddy reward we hope to get, not for some prudential motive that will cause us to be immune from danger which otherwise we might have to face or some pain that we might otherwise have to endure. No, we love him because here is a blending of personality with God. Here is the coming of Heaven. We love him because he, Jesus, epitomises that common service which was expressed for all time when, not long before he died, he girded himself with a towel and performed the most menial of all tasks, a task usually left to the lowest slave. He washed the feet of his friends. That is why we love him. That is why, when Judas realised the crime he had committed, he went out and hanged himself. He hanged himself because he had not the courage to face that love which he had traduced. That is why Peter wept bitterly, and then spent the rest of his life loving his master . . .[18]

When I hear Jesus say to me, 'Take up your cross and follow me,' I must free my hands so that I may hold that cross. I cannot hold the cross while my fist is clenched. I cannot hold the cross if I am already grasping the sword. I cannot hold the cross so long as I insist that I must have also in my hand a written understanding that assures my success. There is a kind of nakedness that belongs to meekness and cross-bearing.[19]

Though we cannot carry our Lord's cross . . . we can and must catch something of that spirit of self-denial in which he 'emptied himself of all but love'. Only so will we be granted an entrance into the meaning of the cross.[20]

The trouble is that though we are glad to go to the wedding feast with him, or sit at his feet on the Mount, to share in the wonder of his transfiguration and even join with him in proclaiming that the kingdom of Heaven is at hand, the day comes when he says, 'I go to Jerusalem,' and then we forsake him. I am afraid that this will be the final condemnation of the age in which we live: 'Our children will take no notice of us that we had been with Jesus . . .' That condemnation will fall much more heavily on those who still call themselves his disciples, and even follow in his train to Jerusalem, but in reality have deserted him in spirit, for our children will see all too clearly that in Jerusalem disciples like that cannot but betray their Lord, even if they do not sell their souls, like Judas, for thirty pieces of silver.[21]

I often think that when Jesus was frustrated, as he was by the faithlessness of his followers . . . it was his hope which kept him going to Jerusalem and his cross. If we cherish the hope that sustained him, we can follow in his steps whatever the crosses and crowns . . .[22]

What God requires of me is that which he perfectly received from Jesus – the performance of goodwill, the persistent intention to seek the good of others. With this he is content . . .[23]

. . . if you will resolve to practise the presence of Christ, to make friends with him, filling up your hearts with Christ-like associations, you will find his kingdom of peace and goodwill springing up in your own life, and then you'll be free to work for it and win the world.[24]

My responsibility as a Christian is obedience, not calculation.[25]

The practice by the grace of God of Christian obedience begins in suspense of thought until that thought can be fertilised by wilful action.[26]

The responsibility of would-be Christians, bidden to walk in the steps of the Prince of Peace, is first and above all to be obedient, rather than to endeavour to modify the gospel in the interests of what they imagine to be practical politics. Obedience is the opening of the door to God's power. That is what the Sermon on the Mount says. God can use our obedience to transform the situation tomorrow.[27]

I am to obey God intelligently and humbly. The consequences of such obedience are not my responsibility but God's. I am to love my enemies; refuse to answer violence with violence and to practise meekness; to live as if God's kingdom were already here; to refuse to give way to fear or doubt. If I seek to do these things a day at a time, I can believe with confidence that God will take care of the morrow.[28]

The kingdom can come because there is a power which operates through our obedience.[29]

When disciples are ready to go to Jerusalem on the same terms as they walked with their Lord in Galilee, that is when in the time of storm . . . God can take every act of those disciples, every blow they receive, every suffering they endure, can charge each of them with revolutionary potency, and through such obedience can bring in his kingdom suddenly and with power.[30]

There is only one road left – it is the road not so much of greater faith in God but faith in a greater God than the God to whom we have been praying. It is faith in a heavenly Father who will give us all 'peace that passes understanding' when we give him our full obedience. It is faith like that of our blessed Saviour who, in the Garden of Gethsemane, prayed, 'Thy will be done,' and who bids us deny ourselves and take up his cross and follow him.[31]

Our failures are due to the fact that we have been unprepared to take the risks which Jesus took and therefore we have not experienced the resurrection.[32]

As I reread the twenty-second chapter of St Luke it is not Jesus who seems to waver in his rejection of the sword. It is we, his disciples, who, by our hesitancy and unbelief, make his agony the more profound. We, instead of facing the cross with him, sleep while he prays and deny him when he needs us most.[33]

The best way to find out about God is still to try out the Sermon on the Mount rather than to think about the Nicene Creed.[34]

The spiritual reformer must become the political revolutionary, and go through with it to the end as Jesus did.[35]

A Christian cannot really be born again . . . unless born into a new political and economic allegiance as well as personal devotion.[36]

Unless we hear the voice of Jesus clear and still – in politics, in economics, in citizenship as well as in the realms of prayer and penitence – unless, in fact, the voice of Jesus penetrates right into the secular and highly artificial life that we live today, then that voice will not be heard.[37]

I commend to you the place of discipline in the ordered life of the disciple, but above all the place of devotion to his kingdom.[38]

I do not believe you can know the truth unless you are a pilgrim to the kingdom of God, as Jesus announced it.[39]

The spiritual valour of Jesus was the power upon which he was able to call to produce the effect which he intended. As I look at him on the cross, and hear his cry, 'It is finished. It is accomplished,' I see the consummation of that intention. He had perceived with absolute clarity what his mission was and he had been able to carry it out perfectly in the teeth of all that people could do to him, because of his invincible courage. He is for me, and for all of us, the pattern, the polished diamond in its true setting, the pure courage of perfect manhood.[40]

It is only when we can say with Jesus, 'It is accomplished,' that on Easter Day we can rise and claim, 'He is risen, he is risen, indeed.'[41]

I take my standards from the spirit of Jesus as revealed in history and perpetuated in his saints.[42]

Prayer

There is no 'easy ride' to prayer – we must be driven to it along the rough road of need.[1]

Prayer is the attempt to put yourself on God's side ....[2]

Prayer is self-consciousness at its height ...[3]

The sublime heights of prayer do not consist in clamouring at the throne of grace for blessings we desire, but in prostrating ourselves before the throne and gazing upon Christ in thought and imagination and saying, 'Not my will, but thine be done.'[4]

Because we are made for God, we will find rest in him; and because we are God's children, then what God wills for us is ultimately the best for us too. And that is the sublime peak of prayer, the royalty of inward happiness, the serenity which comes from being close to God. May we all pray like that.[5]

Prayer is digging a channel in the sand towards the incoming tide – and if you dig it straight and true, you do not afterwards have to lap the incoming tide into the channel. By its own irresistible force it fills the channel and flows along. That is what happens in prayer.[6]

The thing that binds us together when we pray is that we try to see the footmarks of Jesus Christ. And as we see those footmarks, and as we try and put our feet in those marks, then we can pray.[7]

Prayer is not an effort we make to *change* God's will; it is an effort we make to *find* God's will.[8]

... if you pray for people you are putting something into the water which they will drink; you are putting something into the life from which they will derive their vitality. For we do, at a certain level, belong to one another. That is why Jesus prayed for his friends and that is why our prayers may be effective.[9]

God may just as truly be answering our prayers when He says *no*. The Jesus who could not see God through the mist of his own agony, who said, 'My God, my God, why hast thou forsaken me?', is the same Jesus who did not allow his feelings in any way to disturb the serenity of his true prayer life – who went on to say, 'Nevertheless, Father, into thy hands I commend my soul.'[10]

As I reflect on the evil I have committed or the evil in which I have been incriminated, I know that it would not have taken place had I at that moment been praying. The fact of prayer would have stood as a bulwark – as a shield – against the things which I have done that are evil, and the things I have done of which my conscience is afraid.[11]

I am not out for a spiritual stroll when I kneel to pray. I am undertaking a journey to the kingdom of God and I need the equipment of God's truth and God's power if I am to be a pilgrim on that narrow and hazardous way.[12]

At its depth Christian prayer is mind and heart allowing the Holy Spirit to flow in so that as little as possible of our own imperfection and sin and frailty may constitute a barrier.[13]

Prayer leads to knowledge of what we must do.[14]

I'm absolutely certain that what we ask for in the Lord's Prayer we can look forward to with the same complete assurance with which we can look forward to the sunrise tomorrow morning. And surely that is enough to be going on with – to say the Lord's Prayer with confidence and conviction.[15]

[Saying 'Thy will be done'] is the doorway to those profundities of prayer which have been revealed to us by the saints and the mystics.[16]

Prayer belongs to the real world, and wherever it is used it makes a real difference. It changes men and women and it changes things, you can be sure of that. Forty million people who between now and tomorrow night said a prayer intelligently and sincerely, really meaning it, would mark the beginning of a moral revolution.[17]

Holiness

The essence of goodness is initiating what is good, not merely copying what somebody else has done.[1]

Goodness is still the quality without which we can never overcome our crisis, no matter how clever we are, for goodness is not a negative attitude to life . . . Goodness is power – the power that comes from penitence for our carelessness of God and faith that he will help us to live as he wants us to live, in amity and neighbourliness in his world.[2]

A Christian consortium of virtue is a blend of moral values that produce a new sort of human being compounded of goodwill on fire, non-violent activity, meekness and self-denial, and crowned with the quality of personal obedience to a Supreme Being who makes himself known to us in Jesus.[3]

To listen to [Jesus Christ] is to make the discovery that God is asking us to do nothing except to offer ourselves to him so that he can give us goodness and strength to overcome every crisis in ourselves and in our affairs.[4]

The inner life is best cultivated when we think of it as the fruit of a Christ-like husbandry of the soil and seeds . . . of our earthly affairs.[5]

. . . fundamental Christianity is not making up your mind as to whether what Jesus Christ said was reasonable or unreasonable; fundamental Christianity is receiving into your life something of God, something of Christ and the love of God, and becoming a better person, a finer Christian . . . the sort of person who stands out – that is fundamental Christianity.[6]

If we [are] cleansed by Jesus Christ . . . we may still, like Peter, make our mistakes, we may still, like Thomas, retain some of our doubts, but we shall be confirmed and converted, and shall preach the gospel, and make it impossible that Jesus should suffer any more, and possible for that kingdom to come which we have always cherished in our hearts.[7]

We must expose ourselves to the sorrow of the world round us and be expendable for Christ's sake; we must go to the people who need us and forget ourselves in the going. Only in that way can we change the sort of people we are and become more like our Lord.[8]

... to ask that you may be holy, as Jesus did (do they sound difficult words in the mouth of Jesus – 'For their sakes I sanctify myself'?), to lay down one's life for one's friend, to be good that you may be of service to them, to see holiness as the fitting instrument of service, and care for other people – that's the predominant motive. That's the Christian one.[9]

If we try to forge God's signature to our plans they will come to nothing. Our hope is in the supernatural power of God which comes to the lowly, obedient heart.[10]

I mean by the saint the one who can radiate goodness and encourage others to want it and make their effort to discover it.[11]

There is no ultimate substitute for being good.[12]

You can only be good if you start with a framework or a fellowship which will encourage it.[13]

Morality is a mark of godliness.[14]

Morality is the concept of what we ought to be and ought to do.[15]

Ultimately we are moral beings or immoral beings and the question of morality must take precedence over the question of political suitability.[16]

Obedience today is the key to well-being tomorrow. To be pacific, humble, pure in heart, avid for goodness – these are the articles of obedience which govern the future.[17]

Persistence is the supreme mark of Christian faithfulness.[18]

It is the way which the Master took, the way of uncompromising love, overcoming evil by good, winning the victory over the enemy by winning the enemy and vanquishing hatred by laying down our lives for those who would kill us.[19]

What we need is a renaissance of inward light and inward truth.[20]

We ourselves are part of the process which has to be changed.[21]

Unless we can understand ourselves and judge ourselves we are in no position to judge others.[22]

When the true naturalness of the good life is lost, then the spasms of moral asceticism and moral licence take its place.[23]

. . . if the destination of perfect goodness is beyond me, it is still possible to set out on the journey.[24]

Kingdom

The kingdom of peace and goodwill is God's gift breaking upon the shores of our life as a great sea.[1]

True religion is discovering the kingdom of God here in the midst of everyday life rather than postponing it to another realm beyond death.[2]

The all-important thing is to seek the kingdom of God. Nothing else really matters.[3]

It is the theology of the kingdom of God that *must be revived* ... Can we regroup our Christian beliefs about God and Jesus Christ and human beings and sin, and the things to come, so that they are centred upon the kingdom of God? We must, for Jesus has laid that down quite unequivocally.[4]

... the world is a moral order, and character will blossom when its roots are set in the kingdom of God.[5]

What Jesus says is that the kingdom of God is the reign of God in the heart, in the mind and in the world. It is the reign of God here and always. It is eternal and inexorable because its citizenship is spiritual ... And it is hard. It is hard to seek that kingdom.[6]

... the kingdom of God does not come without suffering and sorrow and without the cross ... the kingdom of God will not come when we have thought out some new scheme, when we have rearranged our solid programme ... it will only come when we have made up our hearts and minds that we will follow Jesus to Jerusalem, to the courtyard and to the cross.[7]

The kingdom of God is the first requirement in intention and attitude and posture of those who come to the foot of the cross that they may have their sins forgiven and that they may enjoy the love of God.[8]

Goodness is the by-product of the search for the kingdom of God, and it withers as soon as it is separated from this root, like a branch withers when separated from the vine.[9]

... the kingdom of God, or the idea of goodwill among men and women, is the extension of the principles of the individual family to the care of the entire mix of human relationships. This is simply and explicitly set out in the family prayer which starts with the invocation to our Father and immediately requires us to think of ourselves as brothers and sisters.[10]

The true Church is both the workshop of the kingdom for today and the offer of the blueprint of the kingdom for tomorrow.[11]

Preach the kingdom of God and discover the power and grace of that kingdom in eucharistic worship. This is the viable programme, and the paradox is that the very intellectual doubts which are the chief and final obstacle to the traditional forms of revival are the 'friend in disguise' of the apostolic Church of tomorrow.[12]

The kingdom of God is made up of those who seek God's will and do it.[13]

The contrast in the Sermon on the Mount is not between those who seek security and material prosperity and those who seek the other-worldly kingdom. Jesus is talking about one kingdom of righteousness and peace, of well-being and of personal goodness: a kingdom which is both the spiritual experience of the love of God and a political expression of that love in justice and brotherhood.[14]

The kingdom of Heaven is the world as God sees it.[15]

The Christian ethic for Jesus Christ began in objectives. That is the *expression* in all his teachings in the Sermon on the Mount. For Jesus, ethics were bound up in the search for the kingdom of God, which is a way of life which God will have his children live.[16]

We should see our fellowship of service within the framework of the kingdom of God.[17]

For me the kingdom is the community – the family life of all the world gathered round the hearth fire.[18]

Forgiveness

Perhaps one of the most wonderful things about the Christian faith is forgiveness. Because when we have laid down all our laws and set up all our plans we shall make mistakes, we shall fail, and there will be compromise . . .[1]

I believe in the principle of forgiveness, and regard it as infinitely more important than consistency.[2]

Sometimes in this strange and perplexing world forgiveness is the only law that makes any sense at all.[3]

Penitence and piety are the indispensable prerequisites of peace, and in the name of Jesus we must say so in season and out of season.[4]

Penitence is the first step to hope and recovery . . . because penitence cleanses the mind and informs the judgment.[5]

There is more penitence for world hunger and oppression and apartheid than ever before, and more determination to do something about it. This is the beginning of the rebirth of true religion.[6]

We need a moral revolution . . . an act of penitence for our disobedience to God whose guidance and grace alone fit us to use aright the gifts and good things with which he has filled his universe.[7]

A passion for righteousness is still the fruit of conversion.[8]

A Christian faith without punishment is a contradiction in terms. But, in that punishment, there must ever be a door at least ajar, so that those who reach out for God's forgiveness can find it.[9]

A humble attitude of compassion is probably the way to open more doors than the attempt to discover an absolute standard of justice which evades us.[10]

Forgiveness is a much more absolute concept than perhaps we are inclined to think.[11]

Forgiveness is a process by which the past, if not obliterated, is disregarded as having no further impact upon either the present or the future . . .[12]

Forgiveness is the offering of the hand of re-creation, but it is not forgiveness until the response has been made by those who look to that hand as a way of redemption.[13]

I need to be forgiven because it leads to the accession of power.[14]

Forgiveness is a secondary stage – a follow-up. The prodigal son would not have been forgiven if he had not come to himself in a far country.[15]

Where there is no forgiveness there is no hope . . .[16]

The power of forgiveness that God exercises makes things become different . . . In many cases God takes away the scars. But this forgiveness costs God something, although it is his free gift to us.[17]

Forgiveness is the preparedness to take upon ourselves the role of reconciliation. The first stage in reconciliation is to regard the one who has done the evil as one who belongs to the same family, of which you would like him or her to be a moral social partner or a more worthy brother or sister.[18]

I take my stand with Jesus, who says that if you can apply the profound and deepest meanings of fatherhood and family and motherhood, and brothers and sisters, and family table and hearth fire, you can begin to practise this supreme virtue of forgiveness.[19]

The medieval philosophers distinguished between what they called the nail in the wood and the nail in the flesh. To remove the nail at the expiry of the sentence that is imposed for crime or sin still leaves the hole where the nail once was. The removal of the nail in the flesh, under dire conditions of health, means that, sooner or later, the flesh entirely recovers and is as good as new . . . Forgiveness belongs to that second category.[20]

To let bygones be bygones is not a confession of failure; it is the only way forward.[21]

The ethic of forgiveness is the recognition of a family relationship which is not necessarily broken by the prodigality of one member of the family.[22]

Faith, Hope and Love

Faith

Faith for me is a compound of evidence and intention. In many cases on the purely rational basis I am an agnostic . . .[1]

The more impossible in human terms is the journey of faith, the sooner will you come to the source of that divine energy in which all things are possible.[2]

Faith is very hard to come by and just as hard to obtain.[3]

Faith is a matter of will rather than a matter of contemplation.[4]

Faith is the gateway to knowledge.[5]

Only after you have made the adventure of faith can you go back to the evidence and find it is satisfactory.[6]

The Christian faith is an effort we have to make upon evidence which is insufficient to give us absolute proof. It is a venture we have to make in the half-light, for the full light of knowledge does not shine upon us.[7]

The general credibility of Christianity which may lack persuasive force at one point of enquiry becomes the stronger as it becomes more agreeable at another point. Christian evidence derived from many sources is cumulative rather than contradictory.[8]

The evidence for that belief [that God is our loving heavenly Father] comes to me in so many ways that I simply cannot throw it away because at one point I am still perplexed. It is true, in my experience, that having heard God speak I can bear his silence so the problem of pain, as I see it, is a challenge to my faith rather than to God's goodness. My hope of solving it and my strength in bearing it is with him. The perfect answer is only to be found at the foot of the cross.[9]

If you have no faith, reader, where do you get your hope for going on?[10]

Hope

My faith is largely composed of hope and the nearer I get to the end of my pilgrimage the more I cherish Christian hope. I look for evidences in life which confirm this – prayer, love, beauty – and in the cherishing of these things I go on.[11]

Hope is the substance that lies behind the recovery of faith.[12]

Hope is the bell-wether of other, greater acts of faith and love.[13]

Hope is not something I have to feel. It is something I have to do.[14]

A great deal of what before was certainty now lies within the realm of hope.[15]

Hope is the first ingredient of any kind of progress.[16]

Hope is no substitute for realism, and its validity depends on whether it is justified. In a word, is it reasonable to hope for peace and justice and therefore worth while to believe in them? The answer is 'Yes' because peace and justice do belong to the real world. Hope is the window through which we can see that world, so that faith and charity can become the doorway by which we enter it.[17]

To stop hankering after the past, which is irrecoverable even when we would like to recover it, to stop looking after the future as it is governed by the present and, above all, to respond to the beckoning power of actual power and possible change – such make up the stuff of sensible hope.[18]

I find the moral responsibility of love extremely complex and very difficult and therefore it may be a confession of weakness that I find a little more possibility in the realm of hope because you can't prevent me from hoping, but you can put difficulties in the way of faith that I find formidable and you can reprimand me quite severely for not loving as I should.[19]

Hope is the energiser of love.[20]

Hope broadens out into the world of faith and love.[21]

Love

To me the essential characteristic of the Christian faith in its incipience is this enlargement of the concept of love, not only to include those who are contingent to one another, but also to include those who are the enemies and separated from one another.[22]

When we say [Jesus] bore our sorrows on the tree, what we mean is that though our area of love is so restrictive and only affects us, while our tenderness only extends to a small group, for him the cry of the remotest child pierces his heart.[23]

Loving is not a sentiment, though it includes it. It is not a feeling, though it is enriched by it. Love is an activity. It is something you do. It is goodwill on fire.[24]

Love, as Christ taught it, makes other men's and women's sorrows *our* sorrow, their joys *our* joy. We are responsible to God for ourselves and for one another.[25]

. . . when you lose touch with the fact that we are members of a family then, it seems to me, whatever economic prosperity you indulge and whatever programmes you may evaluate, sooner or later you miss the many-splendoured thing which Jesus came to express, to live for, to die for . . .[26]

The love of Jesus, what it is, none but his lovers know. Not that we may bask in that love, as Peter desired to do on the Mount of Transfiguration, but that we may come down from that mountain and cure the leper and house the bereft and clothe the naked and feed the hungry. That is the meaning of love.[27]

It is not sufficient to have good instincts. It is not sufficient to know the Sermon on the Mount. It is not sufficient to believe that we ought to get together. It is not sufficient to believe in democracy. The only sufficiency for feeding God's children is to love Christ.[28]

Wesley believed that if you love God, if you cast yourself in faith on Jesus Christ, you can have the conviction inside you that what you are doing is right.

You will still have to meet your sorrows; but they will not break you. You will still have your moments of doubt. But you can still have that inner conviction that all things work together for good to those that love God.[29]

God has made us that our lives are largely prepared to receive the seeds of his truth and love. Our own selfishness and disobedience are the slugs and crows that threaten these spiritual seeds, but unlike the world of nature they cannot finally destroy its life, for God's ground is so rich and fertile and protected that, even despite our sins, if we drop some thought about him in our mind and some Christ-like notice into our heart, it won't disappear but it will take root, and if we almost immediately forget about it while we are busy with our daily work, it will grow and flower and bear fruit . . .[30]

You are only required as a Christian to love people, not like them.[31]

The only constructive answer to violence is sacrificial love.[32]

The hope of the future is the non-violent concept of the love of God . . .[33]

Love does not cease to be love when its effects are inconclusive by our standards of judgment. Love does not cease to be love when only God sees its fruit. I have learnt by looking at Jesus crucified to be content to practise that love and not demand visible and immediate proof that it works, and I am beginning to find that such love is its own reward.[34]

Love is a sensitivity to other people.[35]

. . . the true meaning of love . . . [is] compassion practised in community.[36]

Love and care have to be interpreted in economic and political terms in the unprecedented world we live in.[37]

It's only as you love God you know that your neighbour is worth loving.[38]

You can't love your neighbour as yourself until you have learnt what is right and proper for yourself.[39]

We can love where we cannot understand.[40]

Love goes far beyond the capacity of words to express it.[41]

I think there are some experiences in life which seem to defy time. I would say that love does.[42]

The same light of love that shines upon us all is differently refracted by each because none of us is quite like any other.[43]

Soper's Soapbox 2

Dr Soper: We are now living in a very clever world. It is not necessarily represented here on Sunday afternoon. People can do almost anything they want to do. The trouble is they do not know what they ought to do.
   (Hyde Park, 19 November 1978)

Questioner: Which of the seven deadly sins would the team admit to? Or any other deadlier?
Dr Soper: A French actress was once asked about the Ten Commandments – there were too many, she said. There are too many deadly sins. I would like to see them reduced – and violence added as one.
   (*Any Questions?*, 22 January 1982)

Heckler: You're talking politics!

Dr Soper: Of course I'm talking politics. So did Jesus. I'm not representing the Methodist Church – they haven't caught up with me yet.

    (Hyde Park, 7 December 1979)

Questioner: What advice would the team give on marriage?

Dr Soper: A basic religious faith is perhaps the best insurance for the preservation of a good marriage. Sooner or later, when passion tends to dry up or when comradeship has taken its place, the marriage is going to be difficult to sustain. I'm not asking they should all be Methodists, though I should much prefer it, of course.

    (*Any Questions?*, 7 February 1958)

Questioner: Which three gifts would you give a bride?

Dr Soper: Faith, hope and charity.

    (*Any Questions?*, 22 April 1977)

Dr Soper: I had a word with the head of police in Belfast after my talk last night . . .

Heckler: Helping him with his enquiries?

Dr Soper: Especially his enquiries about the kingdom of God.

    (Tower Hill, 12 December 1984)

Dr Soper: Now I think you've had a fair crack of the whip. It's

time other people had a chance to ask questions. I give you one more question – and then, shut up. Do you agree?
Questioner: All right, one more question. Dr Soper, can you tell me, is your name written in *The Lamb's Book of Life*?
Dr Soper: Written in it? It's printed on the cover.

(Via the Revd Dr John Newton, 10 September 1995. Dr Soper had been engaged with a fundamentalist during an Order of Christian Witness Campaign)

The Christian in the World

Donald Soper took the world seriously and the laws which governed it. He was thus open to scientific as well as ethical problems and the impact the discoveries of scientists made on the twentieth century. For him the Christian life had to be lived in the context of this scientific world and faith adapted where necessary, for there was only one truth, even if it was not yet possible for human beings to see it in its wholeness.

Donald also believed in a reasonable universe in which there was evidence of purpose, though he became more and more sensitive to the strange fact of evil, which marred, distorted and maimed God's creation, and especially its institutional life and how it was organised.

Within this creation there were different facets which Christians had to take seriously. There was, for example, the animal and plant kingdom, which needed due respect. Then there was the arena of politics and economics, with its own autonomy and role. In addition there was the vexing problem of the nation state, which often led leaders to wage war on one another. Hence Donald was consumed with a search for peace and spent much of his energy exhorting Christians and others both to understand the gospel of peace and to work for it.

As he responded to the twentieth century he saw the major world faith communities interacting increasingly and therefore wrestled with the relationship of Christ to the undoubted insights and wisdom they possessed. Here two strands in his thinking, the evangelical and the liberal, clashed as he tried to live with the paradox they presented intellectually to him. Donald was clear Christ *was* the Light of the World, yet he felt unable to deny the validity and insights contained in other faiths and had to rest content to live with this tension which, like many others, he was unable to resolve.

He was perceptive too about Marxism, which he saw closely allied with religion because it had an all-encompassing view of the world and both a metaphysic and an eschatology. But because of his sensitivity to the contribution the arts make to culture he was unconvinced by the materialistic interpretation of reality which Marxism often presented.

Donald was rooted in God's world of science, politics, the arts and, indeed, creation itself as well as engaged in a search for peace and more understanding between the world's faith communities because he saw life on earth from an eternal perspective. It was this conviction that gave meaning and coherence to his pilgrimage.

God's World

What makes Christianity good news is the assurance that this spiritual world, which won't let us forget it and which often seems to reveal itself to us in strange and bewildering ways, is the same universe that we see and touch and smell every day in our lives, only looked at from a different angle. It's all God's world – body, soul and spirit; it all comes under his love and power.[1]

People say that the world is an evil place but, basically, it is God's world; it is we who make it evil. There is nothing wrong

with politics, except politicians; there is nothing wrong with
economics, except economists; and there is nothing wrong
with our environment except in so far as we injure it by
accepting its standards, and not imposing our own . . .[2]

I believe that this is basically a reasonable world.[3]

There is in this universe evidence of Purpose. It looks forward;
it moves on; it evolves.[4]

One of the effects of the modern, secular age is that we have
lost the sense of the dimension of evil.[5]

In many respects we have to live in a world where it seems
God is silent.[6]

The Scientists

Scientific discovery does not begin with knowledge, it begins
with faith. Unless a doctor believed it was worth while looking
for an answer to disease, he wouldn't look for it.[1]

There is not a scientist who knows his stuff who would not
agree that metaphysical fantasy is the prelude to metaphysical
knowledge.[2]

The fallacy of the nineteenth-century scientists was the belief
that there was nothing they could not find out.[3]

Matter, time and space are all created entities. We have begun
to understand matter, but the concepts of timelessness and

spacelessness are, let us agree, so formidable we tend to ignore them.[4]

The world in which we live is not a closed system to the scientist, who is constantly making discoveries which fundamentally alter the balance of power and the course of events. Why should it be deemed incredible that in the sphere of human behaviour and social action there are as yet undiscovered and untried spiritual agencies which could in their turn alter the balance of power and the course of events?[5]

There is increased evidence that we have the power to alter the physical world.[6]

Nature is a deal more forgiving than men and women in what it does with its dustbins. The gardener piles up the debris of this year's crop and it rots away . . . The industrialist piles up the debris of this year's output and there it stays . . .[7]

The kingdom of Heaven is a realm of co-operation and peace – every physicist believes that, more or less, as he or she finds unity and order in parts of the universe that can be brought under the microscope. Economists are only too painfully aware at long last that the bread-and-butter problem is only a problem because the means of life are distributed according to sectional interest. They know that the overall picture of the resources of the world is one of sufficiency and reliability – science progresses in proportion to its obedience to such a world-wide view. So it seems with the moralist – the world is a moral order, and character will blossom when its roots are set in the kingdom of God. The firmly true elements of that order are peace and purity, honesty and unselfishness – they are already there – and as we identify ourselves . . . with them life becomes intelligible and worthwhile. This is the great justification of the Christian ethic . . .[8]

We are in a favourable universe – the more you know of it, the more scientists understand it, the more beneficent it can appear.[9]

The scientific spirit is that attitude to life which regards truth as attainable, believes the claims of truth to override any other considerations and considers its methods and its findings to be the property of human beings as a whole.[10]

There isn't a scientist in the world who would go two yards in the interests of infallibility.[11]

Ultimately what we know is the result of pictures we build up when we don't know and the way in which we correct them by the evidence we receive.[12]

Religion and science deal with what impresses you as being there and what defies analysis if you try to describe it.[13]

The persistent and unavoidable question is whether or not what we profess is consistent with the reality we experience.[14]

The best scientists are saying week in and week out, if only people would listen to them, that belief is an essential part of all true knowledge.[15]

Miracle does not mean the negation of a known law but the discovery of a new one. Miracle is not something fundamentally mysterious and independent but an experience which denotes a law or principle which hitherto has been neither understood nor expressed.[16]

The Animal and Plant Kingdom

We still have a long way to go before we can appreciate that there is a purpose and the will of God that flows though the whole or there is an element of goodness which is intrinsic to a world which is infinitely more complex, infinitely more difficult to understand.[1]

I would prefer to believe that the soul is sleeping in the stone, dreaming in the animal and possibly awake in men and women.[2]

Treat animals as if they *had* souls when in doubt . . .[3]

Animals suffer as animals, not as human beings. What is detestable is that we should inflict larger doses of their own pain upon them. What is abominable is that we should take our pleasures at the price of their suffering.[4]

There is nothing living which has not an intrinsic nature in itself and cannot be exploited merely for the purposes of human pleasure or human desire . . .[5]

I cannot believe a daffodil is sacred. I am not at all sure to destroy a bug is to destroy something that is sacred. The higher up consciousness goes, the more respect is due.[6]

If we knew how to behave better to animals, it might be a short cut to behaving better to each other.[7]

If human beings will not feel more responsibility to each other, may they not be brought to repentance as they recognise the suffering they bring down upon the animal world?[8]

Soul can be assumed to be personality. It must be something self-conscious: realisation that you *are*, as far as human beings are concerned. Ants and bees have reached a plateau.[9]

The real world is not a divided world, human beings against each other, people against beasts, or even creature against creature. The real world is the one in which Jesus is Lord of all living and in his love all creatures can dwell together in peace.[10]

The Peace-makers

Peace as a passion is as necessary as peace as a programme.[1]

Penitence and piety are the indispensable prerequisites of peace.[2]

Why should we find goodness works and badness fails . . . unless it was in the universal mind long before it dawned upon ours?[3]

The real problem of our world is the problem of living together. The choice before us is one world or none.[4]

The world as a peaceful neighbourhood is only possible when would-be neighbours put away the instruments which continue to make them aliens and continue to keep them at 'arm's length'.[5]

Goodwill, friendship must be . . . unilateral . . . for the essence of friendship is to give and not to wait first to receive or to wait for the prospect of receiving before you give.[6]

I regard peace-making as a great risk but I regard war-making as a fatal risk.[7]

It is part of the Christian faith to believe in peace. It is an equal part of the same faith to practise it.[8]

. . . only when you have ceased to fight wars, to prepare to fight wars, to think in terms of warfare as a means of social and political change, will the grace of God flow back into your hearts and your affairs and hope revive.[9]

Peace on earth and goodwill towards men and women are the first fruits of 'Glory to God in the Highest'.[10]

We can have peace for all now; we can't have peace for some now and for the rest later. That is God's will and nothing else will work.[11]

Peace on earth comes through loyalty to a person rather than adherence to a plan or acceptance of an idea.[12]

We can only take up the cross in the name of Jesus when we have put down the gun.[13]

The road to peace is one that begins at Bethlehem, leads on to Galilee, passes through Calvary and reaches its journey's end in the kingdom of Jesus, the Prince of Peace.[14]

If Easter actually happened, peace (which is the fruit of justice) can happen and all the risks involved in the non-violent quest for it are worth while.[15]

Will human beings go on this pilgrimage to this non-violent promised land? Good Friday is both the proclamation of non-violence from a man dying on a cross and the good news of Easter Day that it will work.[16]

The quest for an immediate programme of non-violence may be out of reach, but the operation of witness to non-violence is a present possibility.[17]

Apocalypse was hitherto in God's hands. Now we possess a do-it-yourself kit.[18]

There are just causes – it is wrong to talk about a just war.[19]

Peace is the fruit of justice and justice can only be done within a certain political and economic framework.[20]

Human beings are the only creatures who organise to destroy themselves.[21]

It is not a question that war contains crime but that war is in effect and substance a crime.[22]

Loving your enemy is part of loving your neighbour.[23]

Peace is the creation of justice . . . the promise of the optimum benefit for each member of the human family within the context of his or her own ability.[24]

I do not believe you can conduct violence in any way which is commensurate with compassion or with love. You can look to effects which you hope will promote both, but any expression of violence must forsake moral values and must conduct itself totally in the interests of efficiency.[25]

Peace is not the absence of hostilities and the ceasing of gunfire; it is a state of poise and equilibrium, of reconciliation and fellowship. A peace which passes understanding, but which never bypasses it.[26]

The Pacifists

My pacifism is an act of obedience, in the belief that by obedience to God's law, as reflected and shown in Jesus Christ, there will be released into our world power for God's purposes which are now held up because of our disobedience.[1]

I have never been intellectually convinced of the soundness of pacifism. Therefore I can only be a pacifist by using my faith. Some element of compromise is inevitable. But it should not deter us from striving along the road until we find means of applying our beliefs.[2]

When we say we have to use violence rather than obey God, we say in effect God is not at work in his world and our obedience cannot affect the situation. Yet obedience to God is our ultimate duty even when we cannot envisage his victory. So pacifism for me is still a faith. It is *the* faith.[3]

Christianity would never have been seen on this planet if Jesus had taken the sword.[4]

Up to the advent of the hydrogen bomb, pacifists like myself have been regarded as misguided Utopians at best. We have been advised to be realists. Now the boot is on the other foot. The tell-tale signs of madness can no longer be concealed.[5]

There is no hope for any kind of civilisation unless its intellectual and material achievements are matched by moral courage and responsibility in which men and women know what to do with the things they discover, and know how to live together, and know how, if need be, to suffer together.[6]

I cannot but advocate pacificism, I cannot operate it. Pacificism is a personal witness before it can ever be a public programme. It can only become a public programme when enough people are prepared to support it.[7]

The way of the cross, even if it involves suffering, undeserved suffering, is preferable to the way of the gun because the way of the gun only increases the problems which, by faith, the way of the cross solves.[8]

The virtue of the cross is not in the sufferings of Jesus on the tree, for many people have had greater torture inflicted on them than Jesus. The virtue of the cross is that it is the culmination of a process to which he set himself at the beginning of his ministry.[9]

As we renounce our weapons, so it is my confident belief, God arms us with his. And the repercussions of our non-violence must be those of spiritual force. The cross has been and is the greatest weapon humanity has ever known; and there are many others, such as forbearance, forgiveness, restitution, which have not had the opportunity of showing how keen is their edge and how complete is their use. Is not our job to bring them into action in every actual situation as it confronts us?[10]

Christian pacifism is not a series of regulations for conduct imposed on its adherents; it is an attitude of non-violence in the whole of life which releases those who accept it to find their own answer to every emergency.[11]

Soper's Soapbox 3

Dr Soper: Many of the First World War generals brought disaster through their actions.

Heckler: What about Cole Porter?

Dr Soper: I don't think he's ever been in charge of anything except the piano.

    (Hyde Park, 17 February 1985)

Questioner: What tonic would the team advise for an overdose of electioneering?

Dr Soper: A dose of hymn-singing – 'Turn back, O man, forsake thy foolish ways.'

    (*Any Questions?*, 13 May 1983)

Questioner: Is Mrs Thatcher going to Heaven?

Dr Soper: Any Conservative will get to Heaven by a circuitous route.

    (Hyde Park, 11 November 1984)

Dr Soper: I see no light at the end of the tunnel in a
capitalist world.
   (Hyde Park, 10 October 1976)

Dr Soper: Even those who belong to the capitalist fold are
beginning to stay outside because there is not enough
fodder inside.
   (Hyde Park, 5 November 1978)

Dr Soper: The moment you begin to raise the Irish question up goes the temperature and down goes the argument.
   (Hyde Park, 17 February 1985)

— • —

Questioner: What animals would you prefer to be if you were
not a human being?
Dr Soper: (*remembering the earlier discussion about fox-hunting*)
Not a fox! A shark from the point of view of efficiency. A
porpoise from that of intelligence.
   (*Any Questions?*, 2 April 1976)

Questioner: Ought blood sports to be stopped?
Dr Soper: (*on the use of animals for human enjoyment*) I well
recognise the difference between ham and eggs. From
the chicken, it's a contribution; from the pig it's a total
commitment.
   (*Any Questions?*, 16 May 1975)

— • —

Dr Soper: I'm not anti-American. How can you be? It's a mass meeting, not a country.
   (Hyde Park, 17 February 1985)

Dr Soper: The House of Lords is first-rate evidence for life after death.
   (Hyde Park, 10 October 1976)

Heckler: Can you tell me a single country in the whole world that has socialism?
Dr Soper: No, of course I couldn't.
Heckler: Well, then, it's a fantasy, isn't it?
Dr Soper: Well, not a fantasy; it's a hope.
Heckler: It is a fantasy . . .
Dr Soper: Did you hear any of the virtues I ascribed to it?
Heckler: It does not exist in any single country. It will never exist.
Dr Soper: My friend, you really mustn't get into the apocalyptic mood.
Heckler: (*stumbling*) I'm not in an apocalptic mood.
Dr Soper: You can't even pronounce it, can you? (*Laughter.*)
Heckler: I'm not in an apocalptic mood.
Dr Soper: Are you a professional heckler around these parts?
Heckler: No.
Dr Soper: You're a very poor one if you are. (*Laughter.*) What I wanted to say to you is this. You asked me a question about socialism. It doesn't exist, I agree. That is all the more reason why it should. I gave you some of the advantages that would accrue. I didn't say they had happened. Why don't you listen to the answer?
   (Hyde Park, 14 December 1980)

Dr Soper: The *Little Red Book* doesn't butter any parsnips for
any Marxist who wants to get on with the job.
(Hyde Park, 5 November 1978)

Heckler: When we get in power, we'll put you down a mine.
Dr Soper: (*coolly*) I suppose there are places down a mine
where one can preach.
Wag in crowd: He'll start an underground movement.
(From the Revd Kenneth Brown, *Reflections on Donald
Soper*, 11 June 1993)

The Politicians

I do not find politics to be as finally agreeable and satisfying as music, or indeed as religion, but we are stuck with it and a great deal of life is inseparable from it. To despise it is the way of the coward and the quack. To enhance it by bringing it the best our minds and capacities can offer can raise it from a necessary evil . . . to the dignity of a civilised art . . .[1]

There is no such thing as absolute goodness, except in the world of intention.[2]

All problems are finally moral problems . . . Arguments, boycotts, vetoes, demonstrations, government action are all, in the last analysis, attempts to put into practical form an ethical attitude. It is the old question: what do you do about sin and, even more complex, what do you do about sinners?[3]

I do not believe that there is any possibility of final and absolute justice on this planet.[4]

There is no such thing as 100 per cent when it comes to politics.[5]

There is no escape from compromise.[6]

When religion forsakes politics it becomes unworthy and useless; when politics is divorced from religion then it becomes materialistic and violent.[7]

When religious belief dies you do not have a foundation for politics.[8]

The breakdown of religious truth happened a long time ago and has now been joined by the breakdown of political truth.[9]

The final ethics for the government of the world are not seriously in doubt. In the end we must love our enemies and do good to those who hate us. It is the ethics for the interim that are the very devil for the sincere Christian and the sincere politician.[10]

The main business of those who believe in goodwill is to seek to increase the amount of it until it becomes a dominant motive for millions of people. That is why the church is surely right in putting its main emphasis not upon temporary political actions but on permanent ethical ideals.[11]

Better to accept the limitations and compromises that are unavoidable in the dusty world of politics so that Jesus and his gospel may be brought into the market place where they belong and where the Christian victory must finally be won.[12]

The cross is the supreme object lesson for the student of politics.[13]

Practical revolutionaries dare not ignore the lessons that must be learned from that cross if they are to win the battle for peace and justice.[14]

Socialism must rest in a belief in God.[15]

For me socialism is the political expression of Christianity.[16]

The truth is that, like Christianity, socialism has never been tried and found wanting. It has been found difficult and not been tried.[17]

Christianity needs socialism as the practical expression of its gospel. Socialism needs Christianity as the moral philosophy of its practice.[18]

. . . if socialism means the common responsibility for all the needs of each, the extension of the family table so that there is an equal place at it for all because we are all children of the one heavenly Father and, in particular, if these propositions imply a common ownership of those things which must be found on the family table, then Jesus was a socialist alike in his Old Testament background and his New Testament Sermon on the Mount.[19]

Socialists say that justice, mercy and goodwill can operate effectively only within a social framework which nourishes rather than starves them.[20]

Socialism is the political and economic expression of human solidarity.[21]

If you try to fertilise socialism with the mixed economy, you will get no fruit.[22]

I am still fundamentalist enough to believe that common ownership can offer a calculable and predictable relationship between supply and demand and, just as important, can bring the kind of society in which creative leisure becomes the boon offered by the machine and not the Luddite threat which it now appears to so many to be.[23]

I believe in socialism as an ideology in order that I may translate it into butter, bread, jobs, efficiency and, above all, a world community.[24]

I believe that socialism is inseparable from pacifism, that it is impossible to secure a world of justice while maintaining the arbitrament of armed conflict.[25]

The Family of Nations

The nation state has proved too small and outmoded to meet the demands of the twentieth century.[1]

Sovereignty is a word which would have practically no meaning if we lived in a human neighbourhood and were brothers and sisters to each other.[2]

Nationalism is the father and mother of the nation state.[3]

Fascism is the preference for authority over common sense.[4]

The road to dictatorship is very largely paved with the failures and cynicism of ordinary people who lose their confidence in political parties.[5]

I believe that society must recognise that liberty is a secondary virtue.[6]

By its fatalistic and cynical acceptance of men and women as selfish creatures whose very selfishness becomes the raw material of any possible economic and industrial structure of capitalism, society pushed the kingdom of God out of this world into the next.[7]

Democracy only works when people are willing to make up their minds on evidence and not on prejudice.[8]

Original sin and original goodness belong as much to systems as they do to individuals within those systems. It is high time that organised Christianity took the task of thinking about what is the Christian economic system seriously.[9]

I am bound to recognise the force of the argument that morality has a lot to do with circumstance, and particularly economic circumstance, and indeed even the claims made by the Church for 'good behaviour' are deeply tinged with the prevailing patterns of economic needs and desires.[10]

Is it possible to reconcile a life which is full of amenities and rich in blessings with a society full of mutual responsibility and rich in service?[11]

The new world should be built on the basis of the family table.[12]

The love of God demands planned parenthood.[13]

This world ought to be conceived as a home, the goods of the world ought to be set on a family table, chairs ought to be provided for members of that family, and what they need should not be provided for them according to their ability to pay for it, but because it belongs to them.[14]

We live in a world in which there is plenty for all if only we share it.[15]

There is no problem of production if we would concentrate on the true distribution of what God has already made available.[16]

. . . if the various communities of this world were to live a more or less general level of economic justice and well-being, 90 per cent at least of our quarrels would be amenable to argument, and could be resolved without terror or warfare.[17]

The worst thing about unemployment is that it prevents people from giving anything.[18]

Morality is lifeless without the environment in which alone it can grow. If you want people to be unselfish, then create a political and economic framework which encourages unselfishness. If you want a human family relationship, then set up a family table and a hearth fire. If you want a peaceful society, then put into people's hands ploughshares not swords. Above all, if you want men and women to practise virtue, then they must enjoy the initial encouragement of food, clothes and shelter so that they may believe that such virtue is worth while and worth cherishing . . .[19]

Unless you marry rights and responsibilities you will not produce a society worthy to be called a family.[20]

The World Faith Communities

I believe that the best writings and traditions of all religions can help lead men and women to Christianity, and would like to see the Bible for the Hindus containing the Upanishads alongside the Psalms and the Bible of China with the exhortations of the Buddha alongside those of Jeremiah.[1]

We haven't a monopoly of absolute truth and we certainly haven't a monopoly of goodness . . . what we have in the Christian faith are certain unique, unprecedented and new perceptions about human beings and in them a particular revelation of the place that suffering takes when it is embraced . . .[2]

The uniqueness of the Christian faith stems from being rooted in history, in a person despised and rejected and crucified. The Buddhists seek nirvana, where desires are overcome. This is also true of Hindus – suffering is something that is totally undesirable. So, in Islam, suffering is always regarded as something which belongs to the evil world. In due time the all-merciful God will give us relief from it. But the young man Jesus Christ, who died on the cross, embraced suffering as a means of salvation.[3]

Suffering, along with the characteristic of uniqueness, really does specify the Christian faith and distinguish it from all other faiths. Christians of all people believe that suffering can be world-embracing, not just world-escaping . . .[4]

Christians should start by confessing how they have treated the Jews.[5]

The Jews are the most extraordinary human group ever seen on this planet.[6]

We can never repay the debt we owe, or indeed extirpate the crime we have committed, in condemning this magnificent race of the Jews for nearly 2,000 years in our official testimonies in the Christian Church for the greatest of all crimes – that of deicide.[7]

There is not a word in the Lord's Prayer you will not find in a Jewish liturgy.[8]

The spiritual giants, the Buddhas, the Isaiahs and Mohammeds, have given us pictures of God each with its truth and its distortions, but all adding immediately to our knowledge of him – but in Jesus I believe we have the human photograph of God, a true speaking likeness. But even more than that I believe that Jesus preaching, healing, dying and rising again is God himself at work in the world, and I must therefore offer Christianity as the hope of all people everywhere.[9]

There is much in Buddhism and not a little in Marxism.[10]

There is great impudence in anyone who is Christian telling Buddhists, Muslims or Hindus what they ought to believe. I have learnt one thing as a Christian and that is the virtue of intellectual courtesy.[11]

The true light of Asia is reflected light that streams from Calvary.[12]

For the Buddhist the abolition of violence is a way of escape. For the Christian it is a way of fulfilment.[13]

The world-renouncing faith of the Buddhists may indeed provide a way of sanctity and purity; but only a world-embracing faith can lift up a cross.[14]

Christianity is the grandmother both of the prophet Mohammed and of the prophet Marx.[15]

Communism is a religion, perhaps the most closely articulated religion that the world has ever known.[16]

Christianity goes further than communism, since it holds a belief in the classless society of people – brothers and sisters within the fatherhood of God – a levelling up, rather than a levelling down.[17]

Christianity is all the good that communism can show, plus something which communism by its very nature cannot give.[18]

The God whom Jesus loved is not the God of the Koran and there isn't a God at all for Buddhists to worship. Let us by all means work together and pray together and repent together. Let us be humble, but we dare not throw away the Christian doctrine of redemption for the sake of getting together with the Hindus, who couldn't accept it. I believe that Easter Day contains the supreme revelation of God to men and women . . . present it we must.[19]

I believe that Jesus is the Way and the Truth and the Life as no other teacher or prophet has ever been and that the

Church which is founded upon him is the highest and best human fellowship, because you'll find in Jesus all the truest and noblest that you can find in the other great religions, but purged of the . . . elements which spoil those other faiths.[20]

To be a Christian is to learn from the things Jesus Christ put into his gospel what is valuable and true in all the great world religions, and from the things he left out what is false and misleading in them.[21]

For all the goodness and greatness of the other world religions . . . it is . . . by the standards of Jesus that their goodness and greatness are measured.[22]

The best argument for Christianity is not to say we are the cream of the earth and that there is only one path, but to demonstrate the good works of Christian love so that others will recognise in us the fulfilment of their faiths.[23]

Jesus still infiltrates the other faiths.[24]

Jesus is not only the name above every name but he provides men and women with travelling mercies that include and surpass the guidance other great religious teachers and prophets have given to the world.[25]

The Christian faith is the economical representation of what is best in other faiths.[26]

I believe Christianity answers more of the questions and more satisfactorily, and gives more peace of mind, than any other religion.[27]

I hold to the Christian faith, but that grip is finally an act of will rather than the finished product of a mental enquiry. Furthermore, I find the arrogance of those who reject the merits of non-Christian faiths deeply offensive and the defence of Christian theism as the one and final revelation of truth and goodness quite incapable of conclusive proof.[28]

Gandhi follows the Christian life as I see it, though not as I follow it ... It is not for me ... to say Gandhi will not be in heaven. It is my job to see that I am there.[29]

The saints of this world have not quarrelled very much ...[30]

The Artists

The world of aesthetics and the world of moral values cannot be disregarded as if they were unimportant just because they require more than the intellect to appreciate their meaning. On the contrary, they are much more consequential and immediate.[1]

A great deal of music and poetry and art are much truer than those things which can get into philosophical textbooks by way of rational thinking.[2]

The pride of great literature is the sense of satisfaction that human beings can rise to a certain height.[3]

There is the truth of the equation and the truth of a poem.[4]

114

There is a royalty of inward happiness in coming close to the world of imagination and art, and every time we choose that world in recollection, if not in prospect, we are better for the excursion.[5]

We all need a daily ration of beauty just as much as a daily ration of bread if our lives are not to become stunted and warped.[6]

God's purpose for his creation is made possible by the implantation in his children, as they develop, of spiritual qualities which appear not from men's and women's past but by divine intention. The sense of beauty, of music, of poetry belong to this implanted realm – so does a sense of humour. It is there before the joke is told or the absurd happens. To find it, to enjoy it and to be the better for it is a most valuable contribution to the good life in time and, I hope, in eternity.[7]

There has been a shift away from dogmatic theology ... towards an encouragement of modes of meditation, responses to the inspiration of great music and art and, above all, the stimulation of wonder rather than the inculcation of particular propositions about God.[8]

It does not necessarily follow that a work of Stravinsky has no musical merit because on first hearing it, or even after hearing it many times, you cannot grasp its meaning, or its counterpoint bewilders and irritates you. I am not suggesting for a moment that you haven't tried to understand the gospel; but to enjoy Stravinsky demands a special equipment in musical appreciation; catch his spirit and you will then see

the significance of his strange harmonies. So with Christianity:
before its words become intelligible to the mind its spirit must
be captured by the heart.[9]

Only art is not destroyed by time.[10]

Testimonies

One unsuspected aspect of Donald Soper's Christianity was the role that wisdom, that neglected aspect of faith, played in his reflection about human experience. Here he was more in an Old Testament, and Jewish, mould than a Protestant one, for Protestants tend to place immense emphasis on faith as the one virtue needed in Christian life.

As he thought about his own faith he had to come to terms with the doubts he experienced, as did so many others. He never felt such doubt to be negative. Rather he came to regard it as a stepping-stone to faith and, for him at any rate, as a vital and necessary ingredient to faith, almost a balance to it, which gave perspective. Yet Donald was always on the faith side of doubt, increasingly emphasising the need to see life on earth from an eternal perspective.

This belief enabled him to make sense, in part, of life's complexities and allowed him to breathe a purer air, as he knew himself to be in touch with a world of grace which flowed through the Christian community to others. It was a constant source of delight and daring to him latterly to speak about this dimension to his faith as he determined to remain a pilgrim to the end.

Wisdom

Wisdom is not the same thing as cleverness.[1]

Wisdom is that perception of the ultimate truth by which you can make your way along many tortuous paths to real profundity.[2]

The truly wise never doubt that wonder opens more doors than reason and logic put together.[3]

The essence of religion is moral, not metaphysical.[4]

A moral law is only absolute if the prosecution of any method to observe it is in itself absolute.[5]

When in the name of religion you give up the search for the kingdom of God as an impossible quest you've given up religion.[6]

... no religion ... can survive in which emotion is not ultimately guided by truth.[7]

Religion is the acceptance of the wonder of the world in which we live.[8]

To gaze with wondering eyes is very often more important than to look down a microscope.[9]

One of the most dangerous things in the world is to think you have exhausted the meaning of something when you've described it in words.[10]

Many speechless occasions are much more revealing than public lectures.[11]

———•———

. . . goodness is the best psychology.[12]

Accept temptation as the opportunity to be good.[13]

Conscience is that experience in which what we can do can be referred to what we ought to do.[14]

Would-be Christians must recognise that there is nothing to be afraid of except sin.[15]

If there were more bad people in the world than good, we wouldn't be here.[16]

There is nothing more to the advantage of evil as the silence of people who could be good.[17]

If you persist in doing what is wrong, you gradually destroy your capacity to do what is right.[18]

One of the best methods of preventive medicine is to be decent and good.[19]

A great many people have stunted minds because they've stunted hearts.[20]

Sincerity is not necessarily a virtue unless it is related to goodness.[21]

A sense of humour . . . is a marvellous antiseptic for the 'trials and temptations' of this mortal life, and regular doses of this antibiotic can make all the difference between contentment and confrontation.[22]

You can buy pleasure; you can only experience happiness.[23]

———•———

We are all potential philosophers. No one is ultimately satisfied with only facts.[24]

The true philosopher is the one who has found the way though the end is out of sight.[25]

When you ask *why* you are already a spiritual being; when you ask *how*, you need not have any spiritual superstructure.[26]

The very fact that we ask questions implies that we are looking for answers.[27]

I do not believe we will ever find a complete answer to all the questions which come to us.[28]

All life must contain in itself an element of open-endedness or we'd be robots.[29]

There will still be pain in the warp and woof of earthly existence, even when all unnecessary suffering and brutality have been abolished.[30]

Everything we know comes *through* matter.[31]

Men and women need to know what is the meaning of the physical world if they are to know the meaning of the spiritual.[32]

We need other people – parents, children, friends, lovers – in order to be ourselves.[33]

Broken families can sometimes manage something of a hearth fire even if they can't manage a family table.[34]

You can only express your individuality if you've got it under control.[35]

Sooner or later there is no final answer to where individuality ends and society starts.[36]

To save one life does something to sweeten this brutal world.[37]

Enlightened self-interest is not a virtue: it's a vice.[38]

The world is no longer a place where you can settle locally the problems that face you.[39]

The real world of wealth and well-being is what you can do, not what you can get.[40]

The one who gives and the one who receives share a common humanity made up of the gift of the one to make possible the vocation of the other.[41]

There is no such thing as an irreligious community.[42]

I am quite sure that theology generally should be a sort of scaffolding through which we do our thinking rather than a substitute for our own thinking.[43]

Theologically, I believe . . . it's much harder to be deceitful than it is to be truthful.[44]

Unless God is good our reliance upon goodness is a pathetic fallacy.[45]

I can't define spirit any more than I can define love.[46]

Spirituality does not consist in cuddling one another on the assumption that we're God's pets. Spirituality consists in the interpretation of the affairs of life in a way which corresponds with the will of God.[47]

———— • ————

There is no way of acquiring the truth which can bypass the moral obligations of those who are seeking it.[48]

There is always a time lag between truth and its final acceptance.[49]

Fanaticism is what happens when it becomes too hard to go on thinking but you are not ready to discard what thinking persuades you to throw away.[50]

Evil has never been as strong as good.[51]

122

There is an unbreakable unity between thought and action.[52]

Doubt

I've got as many doubts as I have faith.[1]

Doubt is the stepping-stone to faith.[2]

If you haven't any doubts, you haven't any beliefs.[3]

I doubt not because I want to doubt but because doubt is the first stage in the ability to believe.[4]

I have found in my life I can put up with any kinds of uncertainties and doubts and that I can get along without knowing the answers to all kinds of questions, provided I can be sure of a few things ... Provided I can put my feet on a few rocks of fact I can still make headway, though nearly everything else is quicksand.[5]

There is virtue in an economy of belief.[6]

I don't find it easy to believe in God but I find it impossible *not* to believe in God.[7]

I have doubts myself and I hope to continue with them, for they have a kind of vitality about them, and I would not barter them for secure acquiescence which bypasses the truth.[8]

There are still many questions I can't answer and many problems I can't solve. Some of them still seem to me to be insoluble, but I've got enough answers to be going on with, and because these answers seem to work, and because they become more sure as the days come and go, I can put up with the fact that I'm still ignorant about the others. I'm clear about the most important ones, and so the others don't bother me too much.[9]

People cannot appreciate the truth of a religious faith until they have had the opportunity of doubting it.[10]

Doubt is the highest loyalty when it is regarded as the stimulus for further investigation.[11]

The arguments *against* a belief in theism are to me almost as persuasive as those *for* it. Purely from the static and academic standpoint I should be compelled, in honesty, to describe myself as an agnostic because the evidence that comes to me from the various fields of human experience does not, in my judgment, add up to any coherent pattern.[12]

Once accept the reality of senselessness and of evil, it is still the fact upon which all science depends that the world is susceptible of intelligent understanding and, better still, it does progressively respond to moral laws. In other words, the facts of life pose a question rather than provide an answer. Nature cannot prove the existence of God; neither can it deny such existence.[13]

You don't see in nature irrefutable evidence of the love of God but you do find evidence which, blending with other evidence, helps you to find what is true.[14]

The very fact that nature in its most complicated and sophis-
ticated form, namely in human beings, seems to prompt the
mind in the direction so that we would like to believe in God
and his goodness is strong evidence in itself.[15]

I must take the various thoughts and facts, the evidence for
and against the Christian faith, and I must do something with
them – just as I am – not awaiting for either a heart that is
pure or a mind that is free from doubt. I must set out upon
the road that leads to God.[16]

There is no knock-down proof that can satisfy the honest mind
as to the supremacy of Christianity. There is no knock-down
proof to the contrary. I am free to make up my mind, not
by ignoring the evidence one way or the other but by such
application to such evidence of the faculty called *faith*.[17]

We have to have a point where we stand in order to have a
view in the first place.[18]

You need not find all the answers, but you ought to get the
questions in the right order.[19]

I'm tired of people *looking* for answers. It's time we found
some.[20]

Cultivate a love for the truth, a zest for the adventure of looking
for it, which is not pre-occupied with the sort of conclusion you
would like to reach. I declare my own experience in support

of this adventure of the mind. Such an approach (and I have practised it) has resulted for me in a deepened conviction that such an unfettered approach does lead to faith, not to scepticism.[21]

The reply of Christianity to the critic is that unbelief has failed inside and outside the Church. Uncompromising loyalty to the spiritual world alone holds the field now as a practical alternative.[22]

As I see it, the real trouble is that those of us who have been compelled to reject the historic metaphysical framework of dogma because of its assumption of exhaustiveness and intellectual sufficiency are still looking for an equally precise and exhaustive alternative statement. What we must learn is that we must not only reject the dogma but reject the frame of mind within which it has been set out.[23]

Doubt is the midwife of truth and, come what may, the future of the Body of Christ in the world of the twentieth and twenty-first centuries utterly depends on a reduction of doctrines and credal statements by the process of eliminating those which can be shown to be outworn and untrue and putting into the agnostic basket those which are speculative and optional.[24]

The atheist's existence is one of the strongest arguments for belief in God. We are restless until we rest in God.[25]

The forms and symbols of Christianity must be changed and simplified so that the essential gospel can shine forth.[26]

126

The ultimate corroboration of the gospel is the sanctity of those who have followed Jesus. Christians must rest their case on that.[27]

Eternity

All we desire here depends on whether heaven is a 'must' or a 'myth'.[1]

You cannot have a balanced view of earth unless you have a view of heaven.[2]

The prospect of eternity, if no evidence for it, is part of that reality where we *wonder*, but so are music and poetry and the whole world of the arts. The materialist tends to assume that only reason is ultimately meaningful and that a Bach fugue or a Raphael painting is strictly meaningless. I find this materialism especially dubious in the realm of human relationships.[3]

We live in a world both inside and outside ourselves which does not explain itself, and we must look beyond that world if we are to make sense of things. It is only another way of saying, 'I need Thee. O, I need Thee.' We need the resources from another world to put this one in order.[4]

I should regard it as impossible to reconcile the love of God with the fact of suffering if the grave were the end . . . But, of course, we don't believe that. We believe that this world is part of a very much wider existence, and that in that wider existence we can see things in a truer perspective. And in the light of eternity, the pains and sufferings of this present life may seem nothing more than one episode, an episode which can be seen against the background of a life growing in maturity and eternal significance.[5]

I do not believe in eternal punishment; but I do believe in the possibility of eternal choice.[6]

I prefer to believe that a God who is the Father of Jesus is at least as loving and forgiving as a decent human parent. I am quite sure that no decent parent would write off any child and say, 'You've had your chance and you'll never get another one.'[7]

The main point of purgatory is that it always contains a chance.[8]

Hell is a condition where you are able so to exclude the presence and thought of God as to be bereft of any sense of reality and truth.[9]

Eternal life is a quality of life, not an enduring condition.[10]

I believe things that are eternally true and good will be in abundance beyond the grave and so I can prepare myself to some degree by aspiring to those things now before I take up my residence there.[11]

Life before death is an experience; life after death is an anticipation.[12]

I really don't know much about the future, and I tend to be suspicious of the credentials of those who claim to be much more knowledgeable than I am. Nevertheless as I find the past intelligible and significant – yielding certain elements that unify its profusion of information, so I find the future intelligible and significant in yielding certain assurances despite its scarcity of information . . .[13]

I begin with God. The same eternal Father who has presided over my life hitherto will take care of my life hereafter . . . Just as the past speaks of dependence, so the future tells of confidence.[14]

Doctrines about the next world, eternal life and the ultimate purposes of God's creation become increasingly unsatisfying as they become more precise.[15]

In my old age life is not coming to an end because time and space are no more, therefore I'm not sitting around waiting for the drift into nothingness. I can be profitably employed in equipping myself for an exhibition of which the requirement of effective pilgrimage must be something which already is spiritual rather than temporal. I must try to live a 'good' life, for that is the only equipment that I can take with me when I die.[16]

At long last we are coming to see that the Jesus who healed the leper was using powers and graces which we too can use today, that the Jesus who anointed with clay the eyes of the blind and cast out the devil . . . is leading all those who believe in him sufficiently to see that faith in the spiritual world is the solvent of material problems and that mind – or spirit, shall we say? – does triumph over what we call matter. In fact, matter is so fast dissolving into that which is not matter that I begin to fear there will be no materialists left very soon. Jesus Christ was no prophet flaunting some unreal gospel in the face of reality. He was expressing in his life that contact between the spiritual and the material which is has taken us so long, because of our disobedience, to perceive.[17]

If you would find a new meaning and a new sense of purpose in the love of God; if you would recover and deepen your sense of the justice of his love; if you would find a world which is reasonable and intelligible, in which it is worth looking for God, then look beyond it. You will see then that this is part of an eternal realm. And if you would keep your faith calm, and the good that is in you true and unstained, then take every occasion to ask God that you may be filled again with his spirit. And ask that the beaker of your life may be filled to the brim; and that you may be running over with good.[18]

Epilogue: Witness

Let me be like Jesus and let me follow him in spirit. When he goes to Jerusalem let me go with him; when he says 'No' let me say 'No' with him; and when he offers himself let me too offer myself.[1]

The way of the cross is the ultimate renunciation of a life of sin and it 'demands my soul, my life, my all'.

To be a pilgrim along that road is our hope and our salvation. This I would humbly offer as the all-important experience in the Christian life and it is the precondition of the coming of the kingdom of God.

But, without hypocrisy, I must kneel, and so I kneel at the foot of the cross. I kneel with all other penitent sinners, for here is the grace and power that makes me penitent. It calls me to a different sort of life and promises that if I will stay with him on Good Friday, I may be able to rise with him on Easter Day to proclaim with joy that he is risen, he is risen indeed.[2]

It is the goodness of my Lord which challenges my sinfulness. So to face that goodness, to open my life to its warmth and strength, to see it confronted by the sin of the world and, from the bitter struggle with that sin, to see it issue triumphant in the resurrection and the redeemed society is the all-absorbing vocation of the penitent sinner, and the equally all-important calling of the justified believer.[3]

Jesus himself washed the disciples' feet; by his actions Jesus sought to illustrate the need for self-sacrifice and the complete rejection of pride.

Jesus also said the quality of that service must spring from love. Love is goodwill on fire; love is expendability; love is that quality whereby we persistently seek other people's good. Jesus gave his time, service, healing; and finally he had nothing to give except his hands, which were pierced on the cross.

There is no substitute for loving people. It is realising that every other person is the brother and sister for whom Christ died.[4]

I would like to finish with a very simple statement of my spiritual journey. I am eagerly looking forward for every opportunity of truth, because I am sure that anything that is true will enrich my knowledge of God. However painful it may be in the process, I am looking for those things which are good, because I find in the companionship of goodness a way to God. I am looking for those things which are beautiful, whoever fashioned them, wherever they are to be found, because I believe that beauty enriches the thought and the idea and knowledge of God. And meanwhile I am satisfied, out of my own experience, that there must always be a sense of ultimate goodness. I would try to emulate the attitude of the very humble and very wonderful Eastern Orthodox Church, [which], without saying the mind is useless . . . knows that there are things the mind cannot reach.[5]

The end is not death. The end is not injustice. The end is love.[6]

Give us grace, Heavenly Father,
we pray thee,
so that our lives may be built
upon faith which can withstand the storm.

Give to us
that royalty of inward happiness
which comes from being close to thee.

Give to us, above all,
the spiritual wages by which
we can go on until we reach
that kingdom which thou hast prepared.[7]

References

Books and Booklets by Donald Soper

Christ and Tower Hill, Hodder and Stoughton, 1934.

Question Time on Tower Hill, Hodder and Stoughton, 1935.

Answer Time on Tower Hill, Hodder and Stoughton, 1936.

Christianity and Its Critics, Hodder and Stoughton, 1937.

Popular Fallacies about the Christian Faith, Hodder and Stoughton, 1937; republished by Wyvern Books, 1957.

Will Christianity Work?, Lutterworth Papers No. 34, Lutterworth Press, n.d. (three broadcast talks 16, 23, 30 April 1939).

Thy Will be Done, a broadcast address, Fellowship of Reconciliation (New Series No. 9), c. 1939–40.

Practical Christianity Today, Ken-Pax Publishing, 1947; republished by Epworth Press, 1954.

Question Time in Ceylon, the Revd D. Lansdown (ed.), India, 1947.

Answering Back, Epworth Press, 1953 (twelve broadcast talks).

Singing towards Bethlehem, Epworth Press, 1954 (the material in this booklet can be found in *Practical Christianity Today* – see above).

Children's Prayer Time, Epworth Press, 1954.

Keeping Festival, Epworth Press, 1954.

It is Hard to Work for God, Epworth Press, 1957.

All His Grace, Epworth Press, 1957.

Here Stand I: The Place of Compromise in the Christian Life (Alex Wood Memorial Lecture), Fellowship of Reconciliation, 1959.

The Advocacy of the Gospel, Hodder and Stoughton, 1961.

Aflame with Faith, Epworth Press, 1963.

Tower Hill 12.30, Epworth Press 1963 (a re-editing of Donald Soper's first three books – see above – with some additional material).

Christian Politics, Epworth Press, 1977.

Socialism: An Enduring Creed (Third Tawney Memorial Lecture),
   Christian Socialist Movement, 1980.
Calling for Action, Robson Books, 1984.
Soperisms, Brian Frost (ed.), New World Publications, 1993.

Introduction

1 *Methodist Recorder*, 3 October 1985, p. 18.
2 *Answering Back*, p. 20.
3 *Croydon Times*, 8 January 1949.
4 *Methodist Recorder*, 16 February 1956, p. 5.
5 Hyde Park, 19 October 1980.
6 ibid., 27 July 1980.
7 ibid.
8 ibid.
9 ibid., 1 May 1983.
10 'The War for Welfare' in *Twentieth Century* (ninetieth-anniversary
   edition), pp. 28–9.
11 ibid.
12 Hyde Park, 27 July 1980.
13 Tower Hill, 30 October 1985.
14 Hyde Park, 11 October 1987.
15 ibid., 24 July 1983.
16 ibid., 12 April 1992.
17 ibid., 14 December 1980.
18 Homily, Hinde Street Methodist Church, 17 July 1994.
19 *Kingsway*, Summer 1957, p. 24.
20 *Methodist Recorder*, 20 July 1952, p. 14.
21 *Kingsway Messenger*, September–October 1949, p. 3.
22 *Methodist Recorder*, 9 January 1969.
23 In George Hunter III, *Evangelistic Rhetoric in Secular Britain: The
   Theory and Speaking of Donald Soper and Bryan Green*, Evanston,
   Illinois, August 1972, pp. 66–7 (unpublished thesis).
24 The Revd Dr Gordon Wakefield, *Soperisms*, p. 8.
25 *Kingsway Messenger*, April–May 1955, p. 9.
26 Homily, Hinde Street, Easter 1994.
27 Three Hours' Devotion, Good Friday 1980.
28 Hyde Park, 14 December 1980.

29 The Revd Dr Gordon Wakefield, *Soperisms*, p. 9.
30 *Tribune*, 12 April 1968, p. 3.
31 Hyde Park, 1 May 1983.
32 Hyde Park, 7 October 1980.
33 Hyde Park, 5 July 1987.
34 Three Hours' Devotion, Good Friday 1980.
35 *Kingsway*, October 1956, p. 10.
36 ibid.
37 *Children's Prayer Time*, p. 70.
38 From a sermon preached on 19 November 1939, published in *Kingsway Messenger*, 19 January 1940, p. 6.
39 ibid., October–November 1954, p. 3.
40 ibid., December 1955–January 1956, p. 2.
41 St Andrew's Church, Newcastle upon Tyne, 26 June 1986.
42 Homily, Hinde Street, 26 June 1994.
43 *Practical Christianity Today*, p. 35.
44 *Methodist Recorder*, 22 October 1970.
45 *Keeping Festival*, p. 21.
46 *Care of the Elderly*, August 1989.
47 *Methodist Recorder*, 28 December 1967.
48 Opening of Soper's address, Westhill College, Summer 1993.
49 Three Hours' Devotion, Good Friday 1979.
50 *Tower Hill*, 30 October 1985.
51 Hyde Park, 30 May 1982.
52 ibid., 20 September 1981.
53 Report of Donald Soper at Tower Hill in *The Times Weekend Review*, 29 October 1994.
54 Hyde Park, 28 September 1980.
55 ibid., 8 June 1986.
56 ibid., 6 June 1976.
57 *Question Time in Ceylon*, pp. 31–2.

Prologue: My Testament

1 Hyde Park, 27 July 1989.
2 BBC World Service, recorded 23 March 1988 for Easter Saturday, 2 April 1988.
3 Homily, Hinde Street, 26 February 1995.

4 *British Weekly*, 13 February 1958, p. 11.
5 *Aflame with Faith*, p. 139.
6 Hyde Park, 14 December 1980.
7 *Kingsway*, October 1956, p. 17.
8 *Tribune*, 19 June 1964, p. 4.
9 *Tower Hill 12.30*, p. 138.
10 Hyde Park, 14 December 1980.
11 ibid., 5 July 1987.
12 To Michael Brown, *Yorkshire Post*, 31 January 1983.
13 *Calling for Action*, p. 167.
14 *News Chronicle* (abbreviated), 14 December 1953, p. 2.
15 *Christianity and Its Critics*, p. 14.
16 *Kingsway*, Summer 1973, p. 6.

The Christian Faith

Christianity is . . .

1 Sermon, 19 November 1939, in *Kingsway Messenger*, January 1940, p. 4.
2 ibid., May–June 1949, p. 5.
3 *Singing towards Bethlehem*, p. 10.
4 Dialogue with Joan Bakewell, St Mary-le-Bow, 4 April 1976.
5 *Tribune*, 2 January 1959, p. 4.
6 *Socialism: An Enduring Creed*, p. 15.
7 *Tribune*, 18 September 1964, p. 6.
8 *Kingsway Messenger*, 14 July 1940, p. 115.
9 Hyde Park, 30 May 1992.
10 *Methodist Recorder*, 16 September 1976, p. 12.
11 ibid., 27 May 1969, p. 2.
12 *Keeping Festival*, p. 15.
13 To Brian Frost, 1 October 1992.
14 Tower Hill, 30 October 1985.
15 *Singing towards Bethlehem*, p. 30.
16 *Practical Christianity Today*, p. 156.
17 ibid., p. 103.
18 ibid., p. 15.
19 Address, Kingsway Hall, 24 July 1980.

20 *Popular Fallacies about the Christian Faith*, p. 43.
21 Hyde Park, 14 December 1980.

God

1 *Keeping Festival*, pp. 19–20.
2 To Brian Frost, 1 October 1992.
3 *Kingsway*, Winter 1967–8, pp. 23–30.
4 Hyde Park, 3 August 1980.
5 *Popular Fallacies about the Christian Faith*, p. 13.
6 Hyde Park, 11 October 1981.
7 *Methodist Recorder*, 16 September 1971, p. 2.
8 Hyde Park, 19 October 1980.
9 ibid.
10 Tower Hill, 7 January 1987.
11 Hyde Park, 5 July 1987.
12 ibid., 30 May 1982.
13 ibid., 27 July 1980.
14 *Methodist Recorder*, 25 January 1973, p. 3.
15 *Tower Hill 12.30*, p. 101.
16 *Any Questions?*, BBC, 9 April 1982.
17 Order of Christian Witness Newsletter, No. 80, November 1964.
18 *Popular Fallacies about the Christian Faith*, p. 20.
19 Tower Hill, 7 January 1987.
20 *Practical Christianity Today*, p. 51.
21 *Why are You a Pacifist?*, Fellowship of Reconciliation, c. 1960.
22 Hyde Park, 11 July 1971.
23 ibid., 19 August 1990.
24 *Methodist Recorder*, 15 October 1970.
25 *The Advocacy of the Gospel*, p. 77.
26 *Question Time in Ceylon*, p. 19.
27 *Kingsway*, Summer 1957, p. 11.
28 ibid.
29 To Brian Frost, 8 October 1992.
30 Address, 'Peace on Earth', Fulham and Chelsea Adult Education Institute, 13 March 1989.
31 *Kingsway Messenger*, August–October 1947, p. 3.
32 Hyde Park, 20 September 1981.
33 ibid.

Incarnation

1 *Singing towards Bethlehem*, p. 9.
2 *Tribune*, 22 December 1967, p. 3.
3 *Everyman*, BBC1, 3 November 1985.
4 *Tribune*, 28 December 1958.
5 *Methodist Recorder*, 17 December 1964, p. 2.
6 *Tribune*, 18 December 1964, p. 6.
7 ibid., 21 December 1962, p. 4.
8 ibid., 24 December 1954, p. 4.
9 ibid., 21 December 1962, p. 4.
10 *This is the Day*, BBC1, 28 December 1980.

Jesus Christ

1 Homily, Hinde Street, 17 April 1994.
2 *Question Time in Ceylon*, p. 29.
3 Sermon on evangelism reproduced in *British Weekly*, 30 January 1958.
4 *The Advocacy of the Gospel*, p. 95.
5 Wesley's Chapel, 15 October 1992.
6 *Tribune*, 27 November 1959, p. 4.
7 *Christianity and Its Critics*, p. 69.
8 Homily, Hinde Street, 17 July 1994.
9 'Moral Conflicts' in *London Quarterly and Holborn Review*, September 1963, p. 97.
10 *Question Time on Tower Hill*, p. 101.
11 Sermon, 'Lovest Thou Me?', in *Kingsway Messenger*, 31 March 1940, p. 71.
12 Hinde Street Methodist Church, 26 September 1993.
13 *Popular Fallacies about the Christian Faith*, p. 31.
14 *Christ and Tower Hill*, p. 118.
15 *News Chronicle*, 24 December 1955.
16 'Moral Conflicts', September 1963, p. 97.
17 *It is Hard to Work for God*, p. 9.
18 Homily, Hinde Street, n.d.
19 *Kingsway*, Spring 1962, p. 15.
20 Hyde Park, 10 December 1972.
21 *Here Stand I*, p. 17.

22 *All His Grace*, p. 22.
23 ibid., p. 13.
24 From *Time for Worship*, BBC Overseas Service, in *Kingsway Messenger*, May–June 1949, p. 1.
25 ibid., p. 2.
26 *Love and Hope*, Church Services Series 25, Methodist Church Home Mission Division, n.d.
27 *Tribune*, 2 February 1954, p. 4.
28 *It is Hard to Work for God*, p. 13.
29 Hyde Park, 29 January 1981.
30 *Practical Christianity Today*, pp. 23–4.
31 Address, 'Peace on Earth', Fulham and Chelsea Adult Education Institute, 13 March 1989.
32 ibid.
33 Hyde Park, 11 October 1981.
34 *Tribune*, 30 March 1956, p. 12.
35 Hyde Park, 3 August 1980.
36 *Here Stand I*, p. 21.
37 'Death of a Young Man', Good Friday meditation, Thames TV, late 1970s.
38 'New Age for Peace' in *A Risk with Christ*, Fellowship of Reconciliation, c. 1960, p. 19.
39 Interview, BBC, 4 June 1988.
40 Three Hours' Devotion, Good Friday 1985, Hinde Street Methodist Church.
41 ibid., Kingsway Hall, 1980.
42 *Tribune*, 8 April 1955, p. 5.
43 From *Time for Worship*, BBC Overseas Service, in *Kingsway Messenger*, May–June 1949, p. 5.
44 Hyde Park, 11 July 1971.
45 *Methodist Times*, 28 March 1937.
46 ibid.
47 Midweek service, Kingsway Hall, 31 March 1977.
48 Tower Hill, 19 September 1979.

The Pentecostal Community

1 *Kingsway Messenger*, 6 June 1940, p. 87.
2 ibid., p. 82.
3 ibid., p. 86.

4 *Tribune*, 7 June 1968, p. 9.

5 *Keeping Festival*, p. 15.

6 ibid.

7 Hyde Park, 6 June 1976.

8 *Tribune*, 7 June 1968, p. 9.

9 Order of Christian Witness Newsletter No. 80, November 1964.

10 Quarterly Review, Churches Fellowship for Psychical and Spiritual Studies, September 1961.

11 Address, Kingsway Hall, 8 June 1980.

12 *Methodist Recorder*, 23 July 1953, p. 12.

13 'To Chaplains of the Armed Services', reported in *Methodist Recorder*, 7 January 1954, p. 3.

14 Methodist Sacramental Fellowship meeting, reported in *Methodist Recorder*, 30 July 1953, p. 5.

15 *Kingsway Messenger*, October–November 1946, p. 3.

16 *The Advocacy of the Gospel*, p. 99.

17 *All His Grace*, p. 116.

18 Farewell service as Superintendent of Kingsway Hall, reported in *Methodist Recorder*, 3 August 1978, p. 3.

19 Sermon, Easter Day 1977, Kingsway Hall.

20 *Question Time in Ceylon*, p. 11.

21 Hyde Park, 26 June 1983.

22 *Question Time in Ceylon*, p. 11.

23 *Kingsway*, Winter 1958, p. 23.

24 'To Christ through the Bible', in *Christian World*, 18 November 1937.

25 Hyde Park, 22 July 1980.

26 *Big Issue*, 2–15 April 1993, p. 13.

27 Visit of Lord Soper to San Diego for debate with creationists, BBC, 7 July 1982.

28 ibid.

29 'To Christ through the Bible', in *Christian World*, 18 November 1937.

30 *Here Stand I*, p. 18.

31 *Kingsway Messenger*, July 1940, pp. 101–2.

32 *Christianity and Its Critics*, p. 106.

33 *Tower Hill 12.30*, p. 148.

34 *British Weekly*, 1 November 1956, p. 5.

35 Phone-in, 'What on Earth is the Church for?' BBC, 20 February 1986.

36 *Children's Prayer Time*, p. 67.
37 *Methodist Recorder*, 16 September 1965, p. 2.
38 Sermon, 14 July 1940, in *Kingsway Messenger*, August 1940, p. 116.

The Christian Way

Pilgrimage and Discipleship

 1 Address, Kingsway Hall, 15 April 1976.
 2 *Kingsway Messenger*, April–May 1952, p. 1.
 3 Reported by Sandra Barwick in *Spectator*, 12 May 1990, p. 15.
 4 *Kingsway*, October 1956, p. 12.
 5 *Methodist Recorder*, 26 March 1942.
 6 ibid., 16 June 1966, p. 2.
 7 Hyde Park, 14 December 1960.
 8 Address, 'Christians and Russia', reported in *Methodist Recorder*, 3 May 1956.
 9 Hyde Park, 12 April 1992.
10 *Aflame with Faith*, p. 78.
11 *Kingsway*, date unknown.
12 Hyde Park, 14 December 1980.
13 ibid., 30 May 1982.
14 *Question Time in Ceylon*, p. 28.
15 *Popular Fallacies about the Christian Faith*, p. 37.
16 Homily, Hinde Street, 5 March 1995.
17 *All His Grace*, p. 65.
18 *It is Hard to Work for God*, p. 15.
19 *All His Grace*, p. 52.
20 *Kingsway Messenger*, March–April 1949.
21 *Tower Hill 12.30*, p. 155.
22 BBC transcript of Watchnight Service from Kingsway Hall, 31 December 1978.
23 *All His Grace*, p. 80.
24 *Singing towards Bethelehem*, p. 31.
25 Dome Mission Anniversary, 12 May 1993, in *Outreach* (magazine of the Dome Mission, Brighton), Summer 1993, p. 5.

26 *Methodist Recorder*, 16 September 1976, p. 12.
27 In *Unholy Warfare, the Church and the Bomb*, David Martin and Peter Mullen (eds.), Blackwell, 1983, pp. 236–7.
28 *Thy Will be Done.*
29 Dialogue with Joan Bakewell, St Mary-le-Bow, 4 April 1976.
30 *Answer Time on Tower Hill*, p. 114.
31 *Thy Will be Done.*
32 Dialogue with Joan Bakewell, St Mary-le-Bow, 4 April 1976.
33 *Tower Hill 12.30*, p. 54.
34 *Tribune*, 5 April 1963.
35 ibid., 12 April 1963.
36 Labour Party Pre-Conference Service, reported in *Methodist Recorder*, 3 October 1985, p. 3.
37 *Aflame with Faith*, p. 37.
38 Homily, Hinde Street, 25 September 1994.
39 ibid, 24 July 1994.
40 *All His Grace*, p. 33.
41 Three Hours' Devotion, Kingsway Hall, 1980.
42 Tower Hill, 7 October 1979.

Prayer

1 'My Way of Prayer', *Catholic Life*, p. 15.
2 Address, 'One World Week and Week of Prayer for World Peace', Hinde Street, 20 October 1985.
3 Sermon, 26 April 1959, in *Kingsway*, Summer 1959, pp. 18–22.
4 ibid.
5 ibid.
6 Sermon, 'Prayer and the Geneva Conference', 17 July 1955, in *Kingsway Messenger*, August–September 1955, p. 6.
7 Sermon, 'The Foothills of Prayer', 3 April 1960, in *Kingsway*, Summer 1960, pp. 25–9.
8 *Kingsway Messenger*, August–September 1955, p. 5.
9 ibid., p. 8.
10 *Kingsway*, Summer 1960, pp. 25–9.
11 *Kingsway Messenger*, August–September 1955, p. 3.
12 'My Way of Prayer', *Catholic Life*, p. 15.
13 ibid.
14 Hinde Street, 20 October 1985.

15 *Lift Up Your Hearts*, BBC, 24 May 1952.
16 'My Way of Prayer', *Catholic Life*, p. 15.
17 *Lift Up Your Hearts*, BBC, 5 July 1947.

Holiness

1 Hyde Park, 19 November 1978.
2 *Kingsway Messenger*, September–October 1949, pp. 3–4.
3 *Methodist Recorder*, 9 September 1971, p. 2.
4 *Kingsway Messenger*, September–October 1949, p. 4.
5 ibid., January 1949, p. 4.
6 From a sermon preached on 31 July 1940, in *Kingsway Messenger*, September 1940, p. 132.
7 'Why Did They Crucify Christ?', *Christian World*, 1 April 1937.
8 *Kingsway*, Summer 1957, p. 32.
9 Sermon, 'For Their Sakes I Sanctify Myself', 14 November 1954, in *Kingsway Messenger*, December 1954–January 1955, p. 5.
10 *Reconciliation*, October 1951, pp. 184–5.
11 ibid., 7 October 1979.
12 ibid., 28 September 1980.
13 ibid., 28 September 1981.
14 ibid., 11 October 1981.
15 ibid., 13 September 1981.
16 *Socialism: An Enduring Creed*, p. 13.
17 *Methodist Recorder*, 3 February 1983, p. 8.
18 Ordination Service, Bath, reported in *Methodist Recorder*, 6 August 1989, p. 33.
19 *Popular Fallacies about the Christian Faith*, p. 112.
20 'Internal Mission', *Kingsway Hall*, 9 December 1976.
21 Homily, Hinde Street, 26 June 1994.
22 ibid.
23 *All His Grace*, p. 66.
24 *Calling for Action*, p. 26.

Kingdom

1 *Kingsway Messenger*, January–February 1954, p. 2.
2 *Illustrated*, 6 April 1957, p. 17.

3 *Tribune*, 10 January 1964, p. 4.
4 Sermon on the kingdom of God, in *Kingsway Messenger*, February–March 1947, p. 2.
5 ibid., p. 3.
6 *It is hard to Work for God*, p. 10.
7 *Kingsway Messenger*, April 1940, p. 52.
8 Sermon at Anniversary Service, Kingsway Hall, 1 May 1977.
9 *Methodist Recorder*, 3 January 1963, p. 2.
10 *Calling for Action*, pp. 115–16.
11 *Christian Politics*, p. 94.
12 *Methodist Recorder*, 16 June 1966, p. 2.
13 To the Revd Len Barnett, Central Methodist Church, Bromley, 1983.
14 *Tribune*, 22 July 1955, pp. 4–5.
15 *Question Time in Ceylon*, pp. 30–1.
16 *Kingsway*, Spring 1962.
17 Homily, Hinde Street, 26 June 1994.
18 Reflection, BBC Overseas Service, 21 December 1981.

Forgiveness

1 *It's Hard to Work for God*, p. 9.
2 *Tribune*, 11 November 1955, p. 12.
3 ibid.
4 *Kingsway Messenger*, January–February 1954, p. 2.
5 *Methodist Recorder*, 7 December 1967, p. 2.
6 *Tribune*, 20 December 1963, p. 4.
7 *Kingsway Messenger*, September–October 1949, p. 3.
8 *Tribune*, 31 July 1959.
9 *Peace News*, 25 May 1956, p. 1.
10 Hansard, House of Lords, Vol. 519, War Crimes Bill, 4 June 1990.
11 ibid., Vol. 338, Rehabilitation of Offenders Bill, 1 February 1973.
12 ibid.
13 ibid., Vol. 519, col. 1164.
14 Hinde Street Methodist Church, 17 May 1992.
15 Hyde Park, 14 December 1960.
16 *Kingsway Messenger*, March–April 1951, p. 13.
17 ibid.
18 Three Hours' Devotion, Kingsway Hall, 13 April 1979.

19 ibid., 1980.
20 Hansard, House of Lords, Vol. 353, Rehabilitation of Offenders
   Bill, 15 July 1974.
21 ibid., Vol. 518, col. 944, 1 May 1990.
22 Homily, Hinde Street, 30 October 1994.

Faith, Hope and Love

1 To Brian Frost, 18 June 1992.
2 *Methodist Recorder*, 9 December 1937, p. 7.
3 Kingsway Hall, Watchnight Service, BBC, 31 December 1978.
4 St Paul's Cathedral, 15 February 1979.
5 Phone-in, 'What on Earth is the Church for?', BBC,
   20 February 1986.
6 Tower Hill, 30 October 1985.
7 *Question Time in Ceylon*, p. 21.
8 *Methodist Recorder*, 15 October 1970.
9 *Tower Hill 12.30*, pp. 63–4.
10 *Tribune*, 25 May 1973, p. 15.
11 *Methodist Recorder*, 17 December 1952.
12 St Paul's Cathedral, 15 February 1979.
13 ibid.
14 Interview on LBC, 26 December 1982.
15 Tower Hill, 10 December 1986.
16 Hinde Street Methodist Church, 17 May 1992.
17 *Tribune*, 16 April 1976, p. 5.
18 ibid., 9 January 1976, p. 4.
19 To Brian Frost, 18 June 1992.
20 St Paul's Cathedral, 15 February 1979.
21 *Love and Hope*, Church Services Series 25, Methodist Church
   Home Mission Division. n.d.
22 Address, 'Peace on Earth', Fulham and Chelsea Adult Education
   Institute, 13 March 1989.
23 *The Advocacy of the Gospel*, p. 118.
24 Final sermon as Superintendent of Kingsway Hall, 31 July
   1978.
25 In *What Men Believe*, Nauman Neame Take Home Books,
   1957, p. 5.
26 Homily, Hinde Street, n.d.
27 *It is Hard to Work for God*, p. 17.

28 Sermon, 31 March 1940, in *Kingsway Messenger*, March 1940, p. 69.
29 *Methodist Recorder*, 10 September 1953, p. 5.
30 *Lift Up Your Hearts*, BBC, 21 June 1951.
31 Hyde Park, 19 May 1974.
32 ibid., 30 May 1982.
33 Address, 'Peace on Earth', Fulham and Chelsea Adult Education Institute, 13 March 1989.
34 *All His Grace*, p. 81.
35 ibid., p. 82.
36 *Care of the Elderly*, 13 April 1990.
37 Hyde Park, 27 July 1980.
38 ibid., 19 May 1974.
39 ibid., 10 December 1972.
40 Homily, Hinde Street, 9 October 1994.
41 Hyde Park, 12 April 1992.
42 ibid., 30 May 1982.
43 *All His Grace*, p. 82.

The Christian in the World

God's World

1 *Lift Up Your Hearts*, BBC, 21 May 1952.
2 *Aflame with Faith*, pp. 114–5.
3 Hansard, House of Lords, Vol. 273, 1965–6, col. 1051.
4 *Kingsway*, Winter 1967–8, pp. 23–8.
5 St Andrew's, Newcastle upon Tyne, 26 June 1986.
6 Kingsway Hall, Little Chapel, 15 September 1977.

The Scientists

1 Hyde Park, 6 June 1976.
2 ibid., 28 September 1980.
3 Tower Hill, 30 October 1985.
4 *Personal View*, BBC World Service, recorded 23 March 1988 for Easter Saturday, 2 April 1988.

5 *Methodist Recorder*, 29 October 1979.
6 Hyde Park, 1 May 1983.
7 *Tribune*, 12 December 1969, p. 12.
8 *Kingsway Messenger*, February–March 1947, p. 3.
9 Hyde Park, 17 February 1985.
10 *Tribune*, 25 July 1969.
11 Hyde Park, 1 May 1983.
12 ibid., 28 September 1980.
13 Tower Hill, 19 September 1979.
14 *Methodist Recorder*, 1 September 1977, p. 20.
15 *Kingsway Messenger*, July–August 1951, p. 2.
16 *What is a Miracle?*, for Sharon Allen Leukaemia Trust, 26 March 1992.

The Animal and Plant Kingdom

1 To Brian Frost, 24 February 1992.
2 Hyde Park, 28 September 1980.
3 ibid.
4 *Tribune*, 6 January 1956, p. 12.
5 To Brian Frost, 24 October 1992.
6 Hyde Park, 3 August 1980.
7 ibid., 1 May 1983.
8 *Tribune*, 23 December 1955.
9 Hyde Park, 28 September 1980.
10 *Singing towards Bethlehem*, p. 26.

The Peace-makers

1 *Calling for Action*, p. 45.
2 *Kingsway Messenger*, January–February 1954, p. 2.
3 *Tribune*, 15 February 1963, p. 4.
4 *Kingsway Messenger*, Christmas–New Year 1966–7, p. 6.
5 *Christian Socialist* magazine, Election Issue, February 1992.
6 *Kingsway Messenger*, June–August 1956, p. 6.
7 *Nottingham Guardian*, 10 July 1957.
8 *Tribune*, 6 May 1955, p. 2.
9 *Kingsway Messenger*, January–February 1954, p. 2.
10 ibid., Christmas–New Year 1946–7, p. 2.

11 *Singing towards Bethlehem*, p. 20.
12 ibid., p. 18.
13 *Kingsway Messenger*, December–January 1952–3, p. 12.
14 Festival of Peace, *Peace News*, 14 December 1956, p. 1.
15 *Tribune*, 31 March 1972, p. 3.
16 ibid., 4 April 1980, p. 2.
17 *Methodist Recorder*, 27 September 1990, p. 32.
18 In *Unholy Warfare: The Church and the Bomb*, David Martin and Peter Mullen (eds.), Blackwell, 1983, pp. 236–7.
19 BBC National Sound Archives, LP 40701 fo 2.
20 *Tribune*, 4 September 1959, p. 4.
21 Hyde Park, 3 August 1980.
22 Hansard, House of Lords, Vol. 519, War Crimes Bill, 4 June 1990.
23 Homily, Hinde Street, 10 July 1994.
24 Hyde Park, 21 October 1979.
25 St Andrew's, Newcastle upon Tyne, 26 June 1986.
26 Report of the Methodist Peace Fellowship, Gateshead, 12 July 1958, in *Reconciliation*, September 1958, p. 178.

The Pacifists

1 St Andrew's, Newcastle upon Tyne, 26 June 1986.
2 *Methodist Recorder*, 14 July 1960, p. 7.
3 ibid., 6 June 1968, p. 2.
4 Hyde Park, 10 December 1972.
5 *Tribune*, 9 March 1956, p. 2.
6 Address to ecumenical rally in Hyde Park during the Festival of Britain, in *Reconciliation*, October 1957, pp. 184–5.
7 Hyde Park, 7 November 1976.
8 ibid.
9 Tower Hill, 24 March 1982.
10 Article, 'The Strength of Pacifism', in *Reconciliation*, May 1936, p. 119.
11 ibid., p. 118.

The Politicians

1 *Tribune*, 6 April 1979, p. 13.
2 *Here Stand I*, p. 6.

3 *Tribune*, 14 November 1969, p. 3.
4 Hansard, House of Lords, Vol. 518, col. 944, 1 May 1990.
5 Hyde Park, 19 November 1978.
6 *News Chronicle*, 24 December 1955.
7 *Question Time in Ceylon*, p. 18.
8 *Methodist Recorder*, 14 June 1962, p. 2.
9 Hyde Park, 29 November 1981.
10 *News Chronicle*, 24 December 1955.
11 ibid.
12 *Tribune*, 23 March 1956, p. 12.
13 ibid., 3 March 1956.
14 ibid.
15 Hyde Park, 26 June 1983.
16 *Tribune*, 2 October 1959, p. 4.
17 *Franciscan*, June 1983, p. 2.
18 *Tribune*, 20 June 1980, p. 16.
19 ibid., 20 April 1979, p. 8.
20 *Tribune*, 3 November 1978, p. 9.
21 Victoria Hall, Hanley, reported in *Staffordshire Evening Chronicle*,
   6 February 1946.
22 Hyde Park, 7 December 1980.
23 *Tribune*, 28 May 1971, p. 3.
24 Hyde Park, 16 April 1978.
25 *Franciscan*, June 1983.

The Family of Nations

1 From 'Affluence and Brotherhood', in *Views*, No. 1, Spring 1963,
   pp. 33–4.
2 Hyde Park, 30 May 1982.
3 ibid., 13 September 1981.
4 ibid., 28 September 1980.
5 ibid., 10 December 1972.
6 ibid., 7 October 1979.
7 *Methodist Recorder*, 16 January 1969, p. 2.
8 Hyde Park, 26 June 1983.
9 *Methodist Recorder*, 1 April 1976, p. 16.
10 ibid., 4 December 1969, p. 2.
11 From 'Affluence and Brotherhood', in *Views*, No. 1, Spring 1963,
   pp. 33–4.

12 Ninety-eighth Annual Festival of the Shaftesbury Society
   at Kingsway Hall, reported in *Sunday School Chronicle*, 14
   May 1942.
13 Hyde Park, 7 October 1979.
14 To Norman St John-Stevas in *Frankly Speaking*, BBC, 1965,
   quoted in William Purcell, *Portrait of Soper*, Mowbrays, 1972,
   pp. 112–13.
15 *East London Observer*, 11 March 1939.
16 Hyde Park, 16 April 1978.
17 *Methodist Recorder*, 23 September 1963, p. 2.
18 Kingsway Hall, Little Chapel, 15 September 1977.
19 *Tribune*, 25 January 1974, p. 9.
20 St Paul's Cathedral, 15 February 1979.

The World Faith Communities

 1 *The Advocacy of the Gospel*, p. 89.
 2 Address, Kingsway Hall, 19 February 1981.
 3 ibid.
 4 ibid.
 5 *Hampstead and Highgate Express*, 18 February 1982.
 6 Hyde Park, 26 June 1983.
 7 Hansard, House of Lords, Vol. 345, col. 475, 18 October
   1973.
 8 Hyde Park, 24 July 1983.
 9 *Practical Christianity Today*, p. 117.
10 Hyde Park, 19 October 1980.
11 *Question Time in Ceylon*, p. 183.
12 Presidential Address, Methodist Conference, reported in *Methodist Recorder*, 16 July 1953, p. 3.
13 Tower Hill, 30 October 1985.
14 *The Advocacy of the Gospel*, p. 58.
15 *Tribune*, 20 March 1959, p. 2.
16 *Methodist Recorder*, 1 June 1933, p. 12.
17 *Kingsway Messenger*, January–February 1948, p. 16.
18 *Question Time in Ceylon*, p. 42.
19 *Kingsway Messenger*, April–May 1954, p. 3.
20 *Practical Christianity Today*, p. 116.
21 ibid., p. 117.

22 Presidential Address, Methodist Conference, reported in *Methodist Recorder*, 16 July 1953, p. 13.
23 *Question Time in Ceylon*, p. 30.
24 Wesley's Chapel, 15 October 1992.
25 *Calling for Action*, p. 151.
26 'Out in the Open', interview for *RE News and Views*, with D. Hanlon and John Coutts, n.d.
27 Hyde Park, 5 November 1978.
28 *Calling for Action*, p. 147.
29 *Question Time in Ceylon*, p. 66.
30 *Cornish and Devon Post*, 4 September 1943.

The Artists

1 *Tribune*, 17 February 1961, p. 4.
2 Hyde Park, 14 December 1980.
3 ibid., 14 October 1979.
4 *Methodist Recorder*, 10 December 1964, p. 2.
5 Care of the Elderly, 6 August 1990.
6 Lift Up Your Hearts, BBC, 2 July 1947.
7 *Care of the Elderly*, 10 July 1990.
8 *Methodist Recorder*, 30 August 1979, p. 8.
9 *Popular Fallacies about the Christian Faith*, pp. 36–7.
10 *Calling for Action*, p. 171.

Testimonies

Wisdom

1 Address, Kingsway Hall, 29 June 1980.
2 'The Resolution of Fear', sermon preached in St Martin-in-the-Fields, 26 March 1979, in *Tradition and Unity: sermons published in Honour of Robert Runcie*, Dan Cohn-Sherbok (ed.), Bellew Publishing, 1991.
3 *Hampstead and Highgate Express*, 22 January 1979.
4 Hyde Park, 17 February 1985.
5 ibid., 10 October 1979.
6 ibid., 24 July 1983.

7 Tower Hill, 7 January 1987.
8 Hyde Park, 7 December 1980.
9 *Sit Up and Listen*, ITV, December 1981.
10 Tower Hill, 10 December 1986.
11 Hyde Park, 14 December 1980.
12 *Big Issue*, 2–15 April 1993, p. 27.
13 *Pause for Thought*, BBC, November 1987.
14 Hyde Park, 5 July 1987.
15 Three Hours' Devotion, Kingsway Hall, Good Friday 1979.
16 Hyde Park, 19 November 1978.
17 ibid., 24 July 1983.
18 ibid., 19 November 1978.
19 ibid., 7 October 1979.
20 ibid., 13 September 1981.
21 Address, Kingsway Hall, 4 April 1977.
22 *Care of the Elderly*, 10 July 1990.
23 Address, Kingsway Hall, 24 July 1980.
24 Tower Hill, 21 May 1986.
25 *Hampstead and Highgate Express*, 26 August 1980.
26 Hyde Park, 11 October 1981.
27 ibid.
28 *Pause for Thought*, BBC, November 1987.
29 St Paul's Cathedral, 15 February 1979.
30 *Popular Fallacies about the Christian Faith*, p. 102.
31 *The Advocacy of the Gospel*, pp. 58–9.
32 Hyde Park, 14 December 1980.
33 *Keeping Festival*, p. 19.
34 *Care of the Elderly*, August 1989.
35 Hyde Park, 14 October 1979.
36 ibid., 19 October 1980.
37 *Tribune*, 17 May 1963.
38 Hyde Park, 24 July 1983.
39 ibid., 21 October 1979.
40 *Hampstead and Highgate Express*, 22 February 1979.
41 *Care of the Elderly*, n.d., p. 1.
42 Hyde Park, 14 December 1980.
43 *Kingsway*, Winter 1959, p. 10.
44 *Any Questions?*, BBC, 23 January 1987.
45 *Tribune*, 28 October 1955, p. 12.
46 Hyde Park, 20 September 1981.

47 ibid., 13 September 1981.
48 Homily, Hinde Street, 24 July 1994.
49 Hyde Park, 16 April 1978.
50 ibid., 13 September 1981.
51 Address, Kingsway Hall, 18 June 1981.
52 Internal Mission, Kingsway Hall, January 1977.

Doubt

 1 Discussion programme, with Claire Rayner, on virtue, BBC, 28 January 1992.
 2 Sermon, Hinde Street Methodist Church, ninetieth birthday, 31 January 1993.
 3 Hyde Park, 12 April 1992.
 4 Tower Hill, 23 January 1991.
 5 *Lift Up Your Hearts*, BBC, 30 June 1947.
 6 *Aflame with Faith*, p. 130.
 7 Hyde Park, 1 May 1983.
 8 *British Weekly*, 6 February 1958.
 9 *Kingsway Messenger*, July–August 1951, p. 3.
10 *Daily Worker*, 21 January 1955, p. 3.
11 Address, Kingsway Hall, 18 June 1981.
12 *All His Grace*, p. 71.
13 *Methodist Recorder*, 8 October 1970.
14 Hyde Park, 7 October 1979.
15 *Methodist Recorder*, 8 October 1970.
16 *All His Grace*, p. 74.
17 *Methodist Recorder*, 16 September 1976, p. 12.
18 ibid., 20 February 1964, p. 2.
19 *Pause for Thought*, BBC, November 1987.
20 Phone-in, 'What on Earth is the Church for?', BBC, 20 February 1986.
21 *Methodist Recorder*, 25 January 1973, p. 3.
22 *Christianity and Its Critics*, p. 34.
23 *Methodist Recorder*, 9 January 1969, p. 2.
24 ibid., 4 September 1975, pp. 12–13.
25 Hyde Park, 27 July 1980.
26 Address to Modern Churchman's Conference, Oxford, reported in *Methodist Recorder*, 13 August 1964, p. 3.
27 Wesley's Chapel, 15 October 1992.

Eternity

1 Answer in response to questions by Hayley Mills for *The Good God Guide*, Save the Children Fund, 1987.
2 Via the Revd David Cruise, 12 May 1994.
3 *Personal View*, BBC World Service, recorded 23 March 1988 for Easter Saturday, 2 April 1988.
4 At London Mission Conference meeting, reported in *Methodist Recorder*, 26 July 1951, p. 15.
5 *Kingsway*, Summer 1957, p. 11.
6 ibid., p. 8.
7 ibid., p. 9.
8 Hyde Park, 11 October 1981.
9 ibid., 11 July 1976.
10 ibid.
11 *Sunday Telegraph*, 31 January 1993.
12 *Tribune*, 18 April 1969, p. 3.
13 *Methodist Recorder*, 3 February 1983, p. 8.
14 ibid.
15 *Calling for Action*, pp. 142–3.
16 *Care of the Elderly*, c. 1990.
17 'Why Did They Crucify Christ?', *Christian World*, 1 April 1937.
18 *It is Hard to Work for God*, p. 29.

Epilogue: Witness

1 Passion Sunday sermon, Kingsway Hall, 4 April 1954.
2 *Methodist Recorder*, 20 June 1996.
3 *All His Grace*, p. 9.
4 Address at Methodist Conference, reported in *Methodist Recorder*, 16 July 1953, p. 11.
5 *It is Hard to Work for God*, p. 38.
6 Address, Kingsway Hall, 8 June 1980.
7 Kingsway Hall, Little Chapel, 15 September 1977.

The Main Events in Donald Soper's Life

1903	Born Wandsworth, 31 January, and baptised Donald Oliver by the Revd Josiah Flew
1906	Sister Millicent born
1908	To Swaffield Road Junior School. Brother, Meredith Ross, born
1914–21	Day-boy at Aske's School, Hatcham. Involved with School Cadet Force. Captain of school. Accidentally kills a boy at cricket
1921–24	St Catharine's College, Cambridge, to read and obtain degree in history
1924–26	Wesley House, Cambridge, to train for Methodist ministry. Reads theology and philosophy of religion (awarded first)
1926	Appointed to Oakley Place Methodist Church (later called St George's Methodist Church)
1927	Starts speaking on Tower Hill (February)
1928	Works on thesis under Professor Harold Laski at the London School of Economics
1929	Gains Ph.D. Ordained. Marries Marie Dean. Moves to Islington Central Hall (September)
1930	Starts Children's Cinema. Methodist chaplain to Pentonville Prison (till 1936)
1931	Ann Soper born
1932	Present at large rally in Hyde Park to celebrate Methodist Union. First listing in *Who's Who*. Volunteers for Peace Army
1933	Bridget Soper born. Methodist Peace Fellowship founded
1934	Peace Pledge Union formed. Active as early supporter of Dick Sheppard. First broadcast (from St Martin-in-the-Fields, 10 June). Brother dies

1935   Visits America and Canada to talk on peace issues.
        Preaches at his first live service of worship from
        Islington Central Hall. Creates centre for unemployed
        there. Broadcasts series of talks

1936   Dorchester Peace Rally. To Kingsway Hall as Superin-
        tendent to succeed the Revd Ira Goldhawk (September).
        Lives in flat off Edgware Road

1937   With Marie Soper and daughters to South Africa. Tenth
        anniversary of Tower Hill

1938   Operation for appendicitis leads to complications and
        blood clot, leaving permanent legacy. Off sick all autumn
        but back at Kingsway Hall by 22 December

1939   Moves to Hampstead Garden Suburb. BBC *After Tea
        on Sunday*

1940   Within a year four leading clergy, including Donald Soper,
        banned from the BBC because of their pacifism. Kingsway
        Hall becomes rest and feeding centre. Addresses Labour
        Party Conference Annual Temperance meeting

1941   Ministers to those living in underground shelters. On
        till for daily canteen providing breakfast for thousands

1942   Starts speaking regularly in Hyde Park. Agent takes notes
        for authorities of what is being said on Tower Hill.
        Judith Soper born. Kingsway Preachers visit Dorking.
        With others pleads in Trafalgar Square for blockade of
        Hitler's Europe to be lifted to allow in relief supplies

1943   Nearly drowns while swimming on holiday

1944   Plans published for 'Methodist Cathedral' near Hyde
        Park

1945   Kingsway Preachers become London Christian Cam-
        paigners. Becomes Chair of Methodist Peace Fellowship

1946   Caroline Soper born. To Radlett for three years.
        London Christian Campaigners become Order of Chris-
        tian Witness

1947   BBC series – *Talking with You*. Also *People's Services*.
        Visits Ceylon with Marie Soper on month-long mission.
        Briefly visits Australia – becomes vegetarian after visiting
        slaughterhouse. Resigns as sponsor of Peace Pledge
        Union. 31 December first ever TV *Epilogue* (from
        Alexandra Palace)

1948   Kingsway Hall growing in numbers and influence

1949   Returns to Hampstead Garden Suburb to live. Visits
        Canada and Australia

1950   Visits USA. Uproar over statement at Methodist Confer-
        ence about communism and a third world war. Becomes
        President of Methodist Sacramental Fellowship

1951   Visits America, Canada, Australia. Uproar at start of final
        tour over comment re proposed Australian referendum to
        outlaw communism. Speaks at large Festival of Britain
        open-air event in Hyde Park (19 May). Becomes President
        of Methodist Peace Fellowship

1952   Visits America, Canada (Vancouver for mission). Cel-
        ebrates twenty-five years on Tower Hill. Elected President
        of Methodist Conference for 1953/54

1953   Thrown to ground in Hyde Park (February). Leads
        OCW week on Isle of Man (April). Reads speech to
        Methodist Conference after being inducted as President.
        At autumn Labour Party Conference preaches before
        Clement Attlee and James Griffiths. On open-air site
        in Deansgate, Manchester (16 November), to 800 says
        he 'wished the Queen would not go racing'. Uproar in
        press and elsewhere

1954   Silver wedding (August). With Marie Soper visits
        Caribbean and on return forms Friends of Antigua.
        Chairs H-Bomb Committee. Visits Russia on delegation.
        Starts writing column in *Tribune*. Speaks at Spiritualist
        reunion service in Albert Hall. Opposes Sir Oswald
        Mosley in Cambridge Union debate.

1955   With others takes H-Bomb petition to Downing Street.
        Visits New Zealand for month. Doctors insist on cancel-
        lation of all speaking engagements outside London for
        three months. Reported to be suffering from constant
        insomnia. Labour Peace Fellowship meeting at Margate
        Conference with Martin Niemöller, Fenner Brockway
        and others

1956   Visits Polish Methodist Church (May). Preaches in
        Warsaw and visits Auschwitz. Miss Key, his secretary
        for nineteen years, retires

1957   Campaign for Nuclear Disarmament formed – member
        of Executive. Delivers 3,000 signatures to Downing
        Street urging end to nuclear weapons. Invited by

Japan Christian Council to pay visit in connection with 100 years of missionary work in Japan. *All His Grace* published

1958   Becomes Alderman of London County Council. Large OCW campaign in Rhondda with George Thomas, MP. Aldermaston March. Donald and Marie Soper take part

1959   FOR Lecture 'Here Stand I: the Place of Compromise in the Christian Life'. *Papers from the Lamb* published. Takes part in Labour Party political broadcast (autumn). His role in politics much discussed at the election

1960   Christian Socialist Movement founded at Kingsway Hall. Professor R. H. Tawney present. Elected interim Chair. Visits Austria (Oberammergau) with Marie Soper. Three missions (May) – Canada, British Guyana, Trinidad. Yale Lectures, USA (*The Advocacy of the Gospel*). Witness for the defence in *Lady Chatterley's Lover* trial. On 15 July takes memorial service for Aneurin Bevan in Wales. Start of Notting Hill Group ministry (September). Sponsors Christian CND

1961   Visits Canada for mission to McGill University. Twenty-fifth anniversary at Kingsway Hall (May). Briefly visits Spain (autumn). CND Aldermaston March still strong

1962   Father dies. Harold Wilson (Chair, Labour Party Conference) gives invitation to take part in Festival of Labour in Battersea Park. Chairs Labour Party Conference CSM Public Meeting

1963   Earl Lectures at University of California (February). Week-long mission in Nigeria. Visits East Germany. Ill

1964   Becomes Alderman of Greater London Council. Visits Holy Land. Takes part in Crypt service in House of Commons for incoming Labour Government at request of Prime Minister. Goes back to eating meat for health reasons. Becomes President of Fellowship of Reconciliation

1965   Becomes Baron Soper of Kingsway. Takes Labour whip in the House of Lords. Visits Zambia for celebrations of United Church. BBC *Frankly Speaking* (29 June). Speaks at Trafalgar Square Peace in Vietnam rally

1966   Interviewed for Canadian TV series. Elected Fellow of

St Catharine's College, Cambridge. Serious pneumonia. *Desert Island Discs* with Roy Plomley (28 April). Visits USA for FOR

1967   Visits Malta with Lady Soper. Three weeks in Kenya with Lady Soper. Notting Hill Group ministry breaks link with West London Mission. Good Friday service on ITV. Mother dies. Lady Soper in car crash. (8 November) Becomes President of League Against Cruel Sports. Resumes sponsorship of Peace Pledge Union

1968   Visits America. BBC documentary on social work of West London Mission. President for centenary year of International Order of Good Templars. Preaches at service and gives lecture. Operation on fore-shoulder (autumn). Hopes Kingsway Hall congregation can share Holy Trinity, Kingsway, with Anglicans. Takes memorial service for Muriel Lester, foundress of Kingsway Hall and friend of Gandhi

1969   Speaks at memorial service for Tony Hancock. Ill (autumn). Part of roof of Kingsway Hall collapses just after service has ended

1970   Sale of Kingsway Hall under discussion. Letter to *The Times* objecting to World Council of Churches' grants to welfare aspect of liberation movements. Labour Party pamphlet 'Why I am Labour'

1971   First Free Church minister to preach at Sandringham. Visits America. Tribute to the Revd Dr Eric Baker at Methodist Conference. Proposes merger with Hinde Street Methodist Church, other options having failed. Labour Party broadcast on Radios 1 and 2

1972   Visits Egypt with Lady Soper. Trafalgar Square rally (autumn) to protest at Munich killings by PLO. Supports Derry Civil Rights Association commemoration of Bloody Sunday. Controversy

1973   Speaks at hundredth anniversary of Oakley Place Methodist Church

1974   Becomes Chair of Shelter

1975   Becomes President of Christian Socialist Movement

1976   Visits Canada. Opens exhibition on Jews in Soviet Union at Conference of World Jewry in Brussels, chaired by Golda Meir

1977   *Christian Politics* published. Becomes Prominent Supporter
        of Voluntary Euthanasia Society
1978   Ends time as Chair of Shelter. Retires as Superinten-
        dent of West London Mission. Visits Australia with
        Lady Soper
1979   In France on holiday. Opens MHA in former Bishop's
        Palace, Ipswich
1980   Speaks at Oxford Conference on Euthanasia. Resigns from
        Exit over controversial booklet on how to end one's life
        if terminally ill. In Trafalgar Square with Jewish leaders
        to protest against PLO. Ends *Tribune* column
1981   World Methodist Peace Award
1982   Kingsway Hall closes and congregation moves to Hinde
        Street Methodist Church
1983   Celebrates eightieth birthday at Hinde Street. Takes
        part in Oxford Union debate on fighting for Queen
        and country
1984   Visits New Zealand for BBC TV interview with David
        Lange, Prime Minister. *Calling for Action* published
1985   Becomes vice-president of Voluntary Euthanasia Society
1986   Moves to Bigwood Road, Hampstead Garden Suburb,
        from Willifield Way
1987   On *Newsnight* and *Wogan* on run-up to eighty-fourth
        birthday. Last of nearly fifty appearances on *Any
        Questions?*
1988   Honorary DD, Cambridge. Made Freeman of Haberdash-
        er's and City of London
1989   Celebrates diamond wedding
1990   Contributes to House of Lords debate on War Crimes
        Bill. Launches Christians for Labour election appeal
1991   Sister dies
1992   Demonstrates against Bomber Harris statue in Strand
1993   Ninetieth birthday celebrations on 31 January at Hinde
        Street Methodist Church
1994   Lady Soper dies (2 January).
1995   Still speaking at Tower Hill and Hyde Park. Resigns as
        President of the League Against Cruel Sports.
1996   Press coverage of ninety-third birthday as new biography,
        Goodwill on Fire, published (18 January) by Hodder
        Headline. Withdraws resignation as President of League

Against Cruel Sports and is reinstated. Radio interview criticising Queen's comments re guns partly because they came only a few days after the Dunblane massacre. Preaches and plants a tree at the re-dedication after restoration of Hanham Mount, near Bristol, the open-air forum used by John Wesley. Opens the Fellowship of Reconciliation Eirene Centre in Northants. Preaches at closure service of the Order of Christian Witness at Hinde Street Methodist Church. Opens Marie Soper project for mothers who misuse alcohol.

1997   Agrees writings, tapes, videos and books can go to John Rylands Library (in the University of Manchester) to form the Donald Sopher Archive. His speaker's stand (used in Hyde Park) taken to Wesley's Chapel to become part of their permanent exhibition in the Museum of Methodism. Attends opening in London of Methodist Conference and speaks in the open air, though now severely crippled with arthritis.